# Family, Friends, and Faith

## *An Inspirational Life:*
## *Sister Barbara Eppich O.S.U.*

Sister Mary Barbara "Nancy" Eppich O.S.U.
Barbara Eppich Struna

*B. E. Struna*

COPYRIGHT © 2019 Sister Barbara Eppich O.S.U. & Barbara Eppich Struna
Cover Designers: Timothy Jon Struna, Timothy Graham, Heather Struna, Loretta Matson
Edited by Nicola Burnell

Although the authors and publisher have made every effort to ensure that the information in this book was correct at press time, the authors and publisher do not assume and hereby disclaim any liability to any party for any loss, damage, or disruption caused by errors or omissions, whether such errors or omissions result from negligence, accident, or any other cause. The authors' memories of certain events may be different than yours and no unintentional harm was intended in publishing, *Family, Friends, and Faith.*

PRINT ISBN 978-0-9976566-4-0
LIBRARY OF CONGRESS No. 2019903215

*"…God go with you."*

# CONTENTS

*I was raised a Catholic.*

*In my junior year of high school, 1951, I went on a retreat that started me thinking about a religious vocation and maybe teaching.*

*Father Walter Tully told me not to think about it…yet. My senior year was filled with parties, picnics, and club activities, but in the back of my mind was that feeling of what life after graduation held in store for me.*

*Courage was needed to tell my parents. I cried when it finally came out. I'd been warned that there might be tears from my parents, but my advisors failed to warn me of my own. Sometimes news is quite upsetting, but when it strikes home it seems even worse. Mom was happy in a sad way; Dad was thoroughly against it.*

*From this time on, prayer was my only hope.*

*Dad did everything to keep me at home. A new family car was bought, the first in almost ten years, a trip was planned, and a summer cottage rented. I still kept praying. S.M.B.*

Our mother clearly remembered the day my sister, Nancy Rosemary Eppich, entered the convent. She had wanted to say one more goodbye to her daughter and give her a hug, but Mother Superior had stood between them, in the doorway of the Ursuline motherhouse, her face set in stone.

She'd then solemnly uttered, "You have no daughter anymore."

The massive wooden door had closed in our mother's face.

# INTRODUCTION

*Stories are the way into our lives.* —S.M.B.

*M*ost people are curious about nuns. When I was growing up in the 50s and 60s, the sisters' long, colorless clothes and religious communal living usually raised a lot of questions and added to their mystery. I felt special because I knew things about the good sisters that the average person didn't. Even today, I still feel that "I'm in the know."

A few years back, I stayed with Sister Barbara at the Ursuline Motherhouse in Pepper Pike, Ohio, for about five days. They have a few rooms set aside for relatives to stay in overnight. In my room were all the comforts and snacks of home. It was just like a cruise ship, except for the lack of salty ocean and sway of the boat. I could come and go as I pleased, enjoyed delicious meals served to me and even had access to a laundry. It was also very quiet and private. I had hoped to combine some work with my visit. I was in the middle of writing my second suspenseful, historical novel, and I needed to write a chapter in which I had to do away with one of my villains.

Each day, during the meals that I was fortunate to take part in with the sisters, I listened to their stories. Theirs were as amazing as Sister Barbara's. I was impressed with their backgrounds, ministries, and commitment to their religious life. These were strong women. The goodness and kindness of the sisters spilled out in their words so much that I could not kill off my bad guy. By the end of my stay in the convent, I'd decided to only maim him and send him off to prison. On the last day of the visit, the sisters had a good laugh when I told them of my decision.

During my next visit to Ohio the following year, Sister Barbara was walking a little slower and becoming forgetful. It wasn't terrible, just a cautionary observance on my part. I mentioned it to her and was relieved that she was also aware of it. I knew how much the telling of her story meant to my sister and the huge work that went into writing and publishing a book, but did Sister Barbara realize what lay ahead in accomplishing this task?

I went to sleep with a prayer on my lips, asking for our mother's help in writing this book. I woke with the notion that I should co-author with Sister Barbara, using all her hand-written stories and notes. As I was typing on the computer that same morning, I heard a quiet rap on the door.

"Good morning," greeted Sister Barbara. "Ready for breakfast?"

"In a minute."

As we walked to the dining room, I told her about my prayers from the previous night and asked if she would like me to write her book.

She stopped, and with the biggest smile, she said, "Praise Jesus. Yes! I knew you would find a way."

After breakfast, we packed up all her notes, journals, and photos into three boxes and took them to the Post Office to send home to Cape Cod. My next historical novel would have to wait.

*Stories wait months, often years before they are told. They wait until we are ready to tell them. It is in our idleness, in our dreams that the submerged truth comes to life. —S.M.B.*

All the words in italics and signed with S.M.B are taken from my sister's hand-written notes and journals. S.M.B was an affectionate term coined by one of my older sisters, Anna Mae. Most of the family use these initials, referring to the first letters of "Sister Mary Barbara," in their correspondence and oftentimes when referring to Sister Barbara in conversation would slur the letters into 'Smibb.' Using her journals and letters, I hope to piece Sister

Barbara's life together and try to uncover the reason for her choices. In co-writing this memoir/biography, it is my wish that whoever reads these words may find inspiration and celebrate her accomplishments, her ministries, and her love for family, friends, and especially her Christ-filled life.

*I have always enjoyed writing letters to my family and friends. In the years that I ministered in the Catholic Diocese of Cleveland as an educator, I often sent hand-written letters for thank you notes or business reasons rather than an email. I enjoy writing. I have found in my lifetime that letter writing is healing, but sadly, it is becoming a lost art.*

*My sister Barbara Ann and I are both writing stories. When I visit her on Cape Cod, and we drive together, we share the why and the how we have become storytellers. Both of us have a great interest in history. She has been researching Cape Cod and I have been putting together the oral and written history of the people that have touched my life over the years. This process of research brings truths to life that just jump out between hard facts and dates. People, no matter when in time they live, seem to experience similar events, attitudes, feelings, problems and faith. It seems that God's plan is continuously working despite the mistakes and foibles displayed by his people over time. If you want to make God laugh — tell him your plans. —S.M.B.*

## CHAPTER ONE

## HUMBLE BEGINNINGS

*I am what I am because of the people in my life.*
                                          —*S.M.B.*

*D*uring the second wave of immigrants to the United States (1898-1914), our grandparents left their birth countries in the Middle Eastern regions of Europe searching for a better life, as did millions of other people. They each had their own reasons for leaving country, home, and family.

*Home is where your story begins.* —*S.M.B.*

### Maternal Grandparents

Rosalia Horvath, age fifteen, was raped by her employer in the village of Papa Teszer, Austria-Hungary, in 1894. She kept the baby. After five years of raising little Rose by herself, the elders in the family thought it would be best if Rosalia, now nineteen, left with her daughter for America to start a new life. At that time, the few laws regulating immigration stated that you needed someone to sponsor you, and that you had to have a place to stay when you arrived.

Rosalia and little Rose headed for Cleveland, Ohio. They arrived in New York on the S.S. Weimar, April 1899, courtesy of Rosalia's godmother, Marni Sasak, who already lived in America. Rosalia had shortened her name to Rosa and listed $4 as the grand sum of money that she possessed, along with a few gifts from her aunts. One of these gifts was a white linen wall hanging on which they had embroidered beautiful decorative designs and sewn a Hungarian phrase in red letters: *Beke teszi a hazal boldoggia* (Peace makes a Happy Home), to remind Rosa of her heritage.

Michael (Michaly) Gron was twenty-seven when he emigrated from the village of Acs, Austria-Hungary in 1899. He came to America to join his younger brother, Steve Gron, who was already settled in Cleveland. Many Hungarian peasant men left their homeland for a chance to make fast money and planned to eventually return to Hungary. Emigrating from their economically deprived country for more opportunity was on these immigrant men's minds, and the two Gron brothers had the same thoughts.

Michael joined his brother in Cleveland and, according to the 1900 U.S. census, both brothers lived in a rooming house. Rooming houses had sprung up in people's private homes in the Northeast cities, like Cleveland, to accommodate the thousands of men wanting to work. Most took the dangerous jobs that no one else wanted, especially in the steel mills. According to the census, Michael and Steve could not speak English but could read and write in Hungarian. Michael was employed as a molder and Steve as a railroad worker. They were listed as "aliens."

Family stories tell of why the young immigrants, Rosa Horvath and Michael Gron, who had travelled to the U.S. the same year but on different ships, wanted to marry each other. Rosa liked the fact that Michael played the flute. She loved to listen to him as he marched in the funeral processions from their parish church, St. Elizabeth's.

The city streets in 1900 were filled with garbage and animal or human excrement. Women had to lift up their skirts to cross the streets. Michael favored Rosa because she had the cleanest petticoats.

They married on September 16, 1902, in Cleveland. According to the 1910 census, Mr. and Mrs. Michael Gron were living in a rented house on Otter Road. By this time, Michael had become Rose's father and five other children had been born: Frank, Louis, Elizabeth, and Anna, all under seven years old. One child, also named Elizabeth, had died in

1907 at age three. The census information stated that Michael had been out of work for 20 weeks.

A few years later, their seventh child, Katherine, was born. The Gron family somehow managed to buy a small farm on Underwood Avenue, near East 185th Street, in Cleveland. After moving to the farm in early 1914, Rosa gave birth to their eighth child, Michael. On February 19, two days later, her husband died.

*Grandma (Rosalia), (Rosa) Gron had worked for a rich family in Hungary. When the owner raped her, the news travelled to the Boicyi family in America. Her godmother sent money for Rosalia to come to Cleveland and live with them on East 93rd & Buckeye. They belonged to St. Elizabeth's parish. My Aunt, Rose Haffer, was the child born to Grandma Gron from this crime.*

*Grandma met Grandpa (Michael) Gron and they later married. They bought a farm on Underwood and East 185th Street in Cleveland. Grandpa worked in the steel mills in the flats and travelled to work on the red streetcar. One cold night, he missed his train and had to wait in sub-zero temperature for the next train. Grandpa developed pneumonia and died at home a few days later. Grandma (Rosa Gron) had just given birth to their eighth child, Michael. — S.M.B.*

A story told to me by our mother, Anna, recalls the day the banker, who held the mortgage to the Underwood farm, came to visit Rosa Gron after her husband's death. Our mother was only five years old. She had hid under the stairs in the kitchen to listen while her mother spoke to the man in the parlor. Conversation began in quiet tones but soon escalated to stronger words. Her mother was a small, petite woman; her clothes were clean but not fancy. Her hair tied up away from her face and her hands folded across her waist gave her a no-nonsense look. From what our mother remembers, the banker insisted the children be divided up or sold, because she would not be able to pay the mortgage payment as a widow.

This five-foot demure woman threw him out.

*Grandma Rosa Gron was not able to read or write English, but could not be cheated with her money.*

*—S.M.B.*

Over the next 2-3 years, Rosa Gron and her children survived by living on a strict budget. Rosa took in ironing and the children handed over money they'd also earned from working. Eventually, the Underwood farm was sold, enabling Rosa Gron and her eight children to buy another house, close to extended family.

A few other childhood events from our mother gave testimony to the Grons' financial situation. At age eight, our mother had walked two miles to clean a house and was paid in apples. When the apples were brought home, via a wagon, the ones at the bottom of the pile were rotten.

As shoes were at a premium, with seven other siblings, the first one downstairs in the morning would have the pick of the best. Intent on getting the best shoes, our mother once grabbed a pair and quickly pulled them on, only to find two mice wiggling in the toe. As she aged, she had a habit of shaking her shoes before slipping them on.

*When Grandpa Michaly Gron died, the family had to sell the farm and move to Upton Avenue, in St. Jerome Parish. Aunt Rose, the child who came to America with Rosa, was married to Jack Haffer and lived nearby on Westropp Avenue. —S.M.B.*

## Paternal Grandparents

Sometimes there are missing pieces to family history due to secrets, information forgotten, memories confused, or no one ever asking the right questions. Little is known of the beginning of our father's side of the family.

Anton Eppich, at eighteen, emigrated from Tyrol, Austria, on May 3, 1904. He sailed on the Kaiser Wilhelm II steamship from the port of Bremen and passenger lists record that he had bought his own ticket in steerage, and that he was headed to his Uncle Josef Hanover's house, in Cleveland, with $8.00 on his person. He arrived in

New York on May 11, 1904. He never made it to his uncle's house until years later, in 1910.

Pauline Kropf (Kruff) (Konig) was fifteen years old when she left Austria, headed for New York on the same steamship as Anton in May 1904, also with $8.00. She was headed to her sister's house in Brooklyn and listed 'servant' as her occupation. All we know after that is Anton and Pauline were wed on October 31, 1908, in New York. Pauline gave birth to their first son, our father, Anton Joseph, in May of 1909.

The small family is found again in the 1910 census. Anton senior is twenty-four, Pauline is twenty-one but lists her age as eighteen and Anton is a truck driver. In the 1920 U.S. census, his last name changed to Eppie, a mistake by the census taker due to the fact that Anton and Pauline still spoke heavy German. Three children are listed as Anton, Carl, and William (Wilhelm). In my research, this list of children confirmed that this was indeed Anton and Pauline, but again, places of birth were incorrect and also the date of immigration. From family stories, alcohol became a problem with Anton and his dependability became erratic. The oldest son, our father Anton Joseph, at sixteen, had to quit high school and get a job to help the household in paying its bills. Our father had wanted to go to college to become an engineer but the need for family stability outweighed his dreams.

In 1930, the census proves more accurate but still we find answers that are mistakes, as in, country of birth is Yugoslavia, and the immigration of Pauline was 1910, when her first son was actually born in New York in 1909. Anton senior is still listed as a truck driver but not working. When Anton died in 1943, he was fifty-seven. Pauline remarried and died in 1974.

*My grandmothers both did laundry and ironing, Grandma Rose Gron for St. Paul Church and Grandma Pauline Eppich for the Millikins, a rich family in Shaker Heights, Ohio. I remember Mrs. Milliken would send her chauffeur to my grandmother's home, on East 55th Street & Payne Avenue, to pick her up because she liked the way my grandmother ironed her linens. Both grandmothers supported their families through this work. My grandfathers were not around to help raise the children. Grandpa Gron died in his thirties and Grandpa Eppich could not keep a job. The war had made many people suspicious of Germans; no one would hire him, and he turned to drink. Things only got worse until drinking eventually killed him. —S.M.B.*

## Anna Francis Gron & Anton Joseph Eppich – Our Parents

*I am a living historian and want to tell the history of my family to the next generation so that they will not forget what happened. —S.M.B.*

Our mother always told us that in the 20s and 30s, young people went everywhere in groups; there were very few official dates and little pressure of being seen with so and so, just a lot of fun. Anna and Anton (Tony) met in 1930 through friends at Euclid Beach, an amusement park in Cleveland that featured an outdoor dance ballroom. They both loved dancing and it became the spark that kindled their romance.

A story told to Tom Lang, our nephew, by our mother, Grandma Eppich: "Grandpa Eppich brought me home one evening from our date. He had a car and we parked on the street (Upton Avenue). He took me to the door and as he returned to the car, some men came by and tried to get into the car. Grandpa yelled and they began to chase him. He was a track star at the high school. He ran around the block (with the keys) and the men could not catch him. He arrived back at the car and drove off. Your Grandpa was a member of the track team at East High School along with Olympic runner, Harrison Dillard."

A picture of Grandpa Eppich and his track team members is hanging in Tom's house.

After a long courtship of three years, filled with cautionary feelings of losing their individual independence, they married on May 27, 1933. Their wedding reception was hosted for only the bridal party and immediate family at a friend's house where they served a simple but delicious chicken dinner. Anna and Tony moved upstairs into a double–decker house, on Hale Avenue, to begin their life together. They were in love.

*My parents met on the dance floor of Euclid Beach Park. They continued to be ballroom dancers until my father died. They often picked me up as a child and held me as we danced together in the living room and at weddings. —S.M.B.*

# Chapter Two

# Family

*Do not forget the things that your own eyes have seen,*
*nor let them slip from your memory as long as you live.*
*Teach them to the children.* —*S.M.B.*

*S*eptember 4, 1934 Cleveland, Ohio

Hale Avenue was a tree-lined street of double houses. These homes, from top to bottom, were filled with hard working middle-class families; each one eager to live the American Dream. The Great Depression was almost over and the light at the end of the tunnel toward a better life was getting brighter.

Our parents, Anna Frances Gron and Anton Joseph Eppich, awaited the birth of their first child. On Tuesday, September 4, 1934, their infant began to make its appearance but not without a struggle.

The midwife, Rose Haffer, who was Anna's oldest sister, arrived to find trouble. She didn't have to travel far; her home was one street over. Confident that all would be well, she wasn't worried.

But the child, a girl, crowned with the umbilical cord wrapped around her neck.

*When I was born, I almost died. I was black and blue, hardly breathing. They quickly called the doctor, whose office was only one block away, on East 140th. Mom said, "she would have the rest of her children in the hospital."*
                                                                        *—S.M.B*

After Nancy Rosemary Eppich was born upstairs on Hale Avenue, the rest of us were born in a hospital: Patricia Ann came next in 1937; Anna Mae, 1939; Michael Anton, 1944; Barbara Ann, 1947.

For the new Eppich family, married life was not any different than it was for other struggling couples in 1934, except for the fact that Tony was lucky enough to have a car and a steady government job at the United States Post Office at minimum wage. Anna had been working as a seamstress at The Richmond Bros. before they were married. When she became pregnant with their first child, she slowly cut back her hours. She managed to work until she reached her eighth month of pregnancy and then quit. Life was good.

With the arrival of baby girl #2, Patricia Ann, in 1937, jobs were even scarcer because the United States had entered a recession, but our father had maintained his secure job. Thankfully, their finances were holding steady on one salary.

Soon, our mother began to have doubts over her ability to deal with two small children. Our father had held on to his independence and seemed to be gone all the time. He was athletic and enjoyed playing tennis every weekend at Gordon Park, and bowling in the evenings. This left our mother to tend to the children alone. Anna was feeling isolated.

*Aunt Betty Dries (Anna's older sister) lost her children at birth and almost died each time. Grandma Rosa Gron and Aunt Katy (Anna's younger sister) would take the train to Chicago and take care of her. In October 1937, Aunt Katy took me to Chicago when my mother was expecting my sister Pat, who was born on November 2, 1937. I was three years old, it was cold and I did not know why I was going on the train. Mom was afraid that she would not be able to take care of a new baby and me. Grandma Rosa Gron would have taken care of me but Aunt Ethel (a new daughter in-law) was also expecting a baby. I do not remember too many things of this early time, but I did know my Mom and Dad really loved me.*

*I was angry when I returned home and found my mother holding a new baby. I also recall a visit from my great-aunt Gron shortly after. It was chilly and rainy. The entrance to our upstairs was an enclosed damp and musty stairway. Great-aunt Gron brought me a rag doll that she'd made. I do not remember what happened during the visit, only what happened as my great-aunt walked down the stairs to leave. As she turned around and waved goodbye, I threw the rag doll down the stairs at her. My mother was furious as she held my new sister in her arms and insisted that I say I was sorry. I guess I did. —S.M.B.*

With the coming of a third child, our parents began looking for a single home in 1938. They were able to buy a house at 1228 East 173rd Street in Cleveland with the help of our mother's godmother, Anastasia Gron, which had three bedrooms and a big yard for playing. The birth of our third sister, Anna Mae, in January 1939, seemed to send our mother deeper into depression, even though she loved us all.

From experience, having two children under the age of three at the same time is challenging, no matter the decade you're living in. And yet, we survive, and our children grow up. Sometimes a faith in God's love gives us a boost along the way or we get a little extra help from the medical profession.

*In 1942, I was eight years old. Mom, my two sisters, and I took the train to Chicago. It was wartime, so a lot of service men were on the train. Aunt Betty paid for the doctor Mom was scheduled to see for her sadness. Mom made outfits for us with hats to match; pink skirts, white blouses, and pink jumpers. Being in Chicago was always fun. We stayed three months. —S.M.B.*

From what I remember our mother telling me, there were many times when our father was not around, but after her Chicago trip in 1942, they both worked harder to keep their marriage together. Life was getting better but occasionally, problems would recur.

*Dad would go for long walks and Mom would worry about where he was. —S.M.B.*

My older sister, Anna Mae, remembered that when she was three or four, our mother left for a walk by herself in the morning and didn't return until evening. Anna Mae had asked our father where she had gone. He'd told her he didn't know and wasn't sure if she would come back. For as little as our sister was, this hurt, and she grew angry with our mother, keeping it inside for a long time. Strange, how some moments stay with us forever.

When I was born, my mother and father were thirty-eight years old. Sister Barbara was thirteen, Patricia Ann was ten, Anna Mae was eight, and my brother Michael was three years old.

Ten years separated Sister Barbara's birth from our brother and thirteen from mine. The parenting skills of our parents, with the three older sisters and my brother and me, became quite dissimilar. When

Sister Barbara and I talked about our mom and dad,
I frequently said, "I don't remember them ever
doing that..." It was almost as if a different set of
parents had raised the three older girls and then my
brother and me.

*In the 1940s, the women always wore dresses and
blouses. Everyone shared. My mom would make breaded
veal and chicken sliced thin. We all loved it. One example
of my mom's creativity was how she organized a play with
the neighborhood children; our living room became the
stage, the porch where the audience sat. Children were
always coming to play.*

*Dad made a big gate that was on wheels to open and
close the driveway. It was a safe place, and Mom could
hear us in the house. We used wood from the garage to
make buildings, magic shops, pretend houses, jungles.
Mom would bring out Kool-aid and cookies for a snack
under the big pear tree. If Mom or Dad sat on the front
porch we could play on the sidewalk. We were only
allowed to ride our bikes, run, or play between the
lamppost and a fireplug on our street.*

*Many fun things in our family life included walking
to Race's Dairy for ice cream after supper and sitting on
the couch in front of the fireplace with Mom reading us a
story. TV did not invade our home until I was a
sophomore in high school, in 1950. —S.M.B.*

What never changed was our parents' deep love
for all five of us. Their rules essentially stayed the

same, but as years went by and the culture changed, it seemed they were occasionally a little more lenient with their last two children. We still went to Mass as a family on Sundays and Holy Days and we observed all of the traditional rules of the Church. When television made its appearance in our house, my father was always the first to want the latest electronic gadget in music or entertainment to the delight of all of us, including my mother.

*A quiet evening at home is Dad's favorite pastime, although he hardly ever enjoys one. If we have places to go, Dad is on the job to chauffeur us. A little coaxing might be necessary if the requests interrupt his evening paper, but after a few mumbles or grumbles, he usually agrees. If Dad is in the mood, he can do most anything and does it to perfection. His ability to take charge of any household duty when Mom is not home is quite amazing. He subscribed to Popular Mechanics and was able to fix and repair almost anything. He is now an experienced babysitter, chef, and occasional laundry expert. Even though he is a carpenter, plumber, electrician, and painter, it takes a few days to convince Dad that a certain job needs the use of his talents.*

*Mom was determined in all she did. She was playful, loving, athletic, helpful, and caring, a good friend to many. My recollections from early days are mostly from photographs and home movies that my Dad began collecting in the 40s. He was an amateur photographer and would develop his own film in our basement. As a family, we lived paycheck to paycheck, with Dad as the breadwinner and Mom as the strict budgeter. Our home was always beautiful and comfortable.*

—Essay written by *S.M.B.* while she attended college as a religious sister.

By 1955, Sister Barbara was living at the convent, Patricia Ann was eighteen, Anna Mae was sixteen, Michael was eleven and I was eight years old. Our father was working three jobs to support the costs of a Catholic education with college on the horizon for all of us. There were school uniforms, gym uniforms, and more uniforms, even black and white oxford shoes for the two older girls in high school, tuition, book fees, and whatever else was needed to stay in a Catholic environment. My mother went to work sewing part-time. This was unheard of, at that time, for a woman with children to work outside of the home. My brother and I became latchkey kids. We would take a bus home from school for lunch, clean up the house, then race to catch the bus back to school. Sometimes we missed it and had to walk the two miles. We usually made it in time for the bell. Mom would always be home around 3:00 p.m.

*On school holidays, Mom would pack a lunch and we would walk along the creek near Villa Angela to Lake Erie – Wildwood Park – and eat lunch on the beach. After work on nice evenings, Dad would take us for a drive up Ivanhoe and Belvoir to pick blackberries along the road.*

*Often, we went to see a movie at the drive-in in Warrensville Heights on Mayfield Road.* —S.M.B.

I also remember those long walks on vacation days. Drive-ins were always special. We would get dressed in pajamas, bring popcorn, drinks, and plenty of pillows. We were all tired when Dad drove us home. I would lie across the ledge of the back window of the sedan and watch the stars fly by. Dad would carry me, the smallest one, to bed. Family fun time never changed as we all grew. Our parents kept us laughing and their love for the outdoors – baseball, long walks, music, and dance – remained with us through the years.

*In my life, so far, I have tried to take one day at a time. I am the oldest in my family of four girls and one boy. Mom and Dad took the time to knit us into a strong and loving family. Mom would not let us go to bed at night mad at each other. We had to 'make up' and say we were sorry so that we could start over the next day.* —S.M.B.

## Chapter Three

## A New Way of Life

*T*eaching would be hard but office work seemed boring. High school graduation set me thinking about my future. Being a telephone operator since the beginning of my senior year of high school seemed quite promising. Due to a wonderful mom, a neat appearance, a willingness to learn, and a happy disposition, my progress advanced rapidly as a telephone operator.

All this should have added up to a successful job for the future, but I still was not fully satisfied. Working with people face-to-face appeared more interesting than just by voice. I thought teaching would be the place to work with people. The increased demand for teachers confirmed my ideas. I liked to care for children and seemed to be patient with them, thus making me more willing to give myself a teaching career. Having been educated by Ursulines, I was impressed with their friendliness and helpfulness.

*My love for the Church pushed me further in my choice of becoming an Ursuline sister. —S.M.B.*

## September 1952

*The last day at home was a family affair. It was sad and happy at the same time. I changed my outfit every few hours. My last dress was the black one. I drove the family to the convent for the last time. When the supper bell rang, I said goodbye not only to my family but also to my short but happy life of 18 years in the world. Then I began my long life, just as happy and even more so, knowing that it would last not only for this life but also until all eternity. —S.M.B*

## September 8, 1952

At 5:30 a.m., the harsh clanging of a large silver bell woke Nancy Eppich along with fifteen fellow postulants. The young women stirred in beds that lined the exterior walls of two dormitory-style rooms.

Hurry up and wait was the order that started their day. Yawning and drowsy, they waited in the hallway for the bathroom, which had only four toilets, to wash and dress. Once they had donned their postulant habit of black ruffled cap, skirt, blouse with a white pepperlin collar, nylons, and thick-heeled black shoes, the postulants made their way to the wooden pews of the chapel and sat as a group waiting for the Celebration of Mass to begin. After two hours of prayer, they could finally eat.

During the first six months of this routine, they were introduced to the Order of Saint Angela and studied in-depth the mission that Angela had set out for them to follow. Soon a choice needed to be made. Would they stay in the convent or leave? Most stayed. Sister Barbara recalls that two twin girls left because they decided to be nurses instead of teachers. The Ursulines were teachers.

*As I met the other girls who had entered, there were so many happy ones that I decided to stay and be as happy as they were. —S.M.B.*

Early memories of my oldest sister and her choice of becoming an Ursuline sister were limited because, in 1952, I was only five years old. I do remember visiting her every Sunday. I was usually bored as the family sat in a circle on wooden folding chairs in the gym of Villa Angela Academy, a high school for girls, connected to the motherhouse of the sisters. The other postulants also sat in individual circles with their families. There wasn't much to do but talk. If the weather was nice, we could go outside on the grounds of the school. There's a photograph of our family standing in a semi-circle on the grass around the sister who never came home and is dressed in funny clothes. I am in the front holding my doll.

## March 7, 1953 – Six months later

The Clothing Day Ceremony was the next step in the journey to becoming an Ursuline sister. After six months of study and soul-searching, the postulants, if they decided to stay, became 'white veils' or 'novices.' They would also take their first vow and be given new names. Nancy Rosemary Eppich became Sister Mary Barbara. This name was available because a Sister Barbara had recently passed away and coincidently, it also happened to be my name. Her legal name on all documents still remained Nancy Rosemary Eppich.

That morning, the postulants were presented with new habits that had been previously sewn and prepared for this special day. Gone were the black skirts and blouses. Now they wore white veils and were called novices. Their daily dress consisted of a long black tunic gathered with a leather belt around the waist. Their head and shoulders were covered with a white, stiff, starched wimple and then topped with a white veil, all attached with straight pins. They wore a slip or 'cot dress' underneath. These underslips were made from the colorful cotton sacks that previously held the kitchen's staples of flour, sugar, and rice. Their morning routines now became longer with all the extra clothing and daily activities that had to be adjusted to accommodate the stiff and cumbersome habit. To add to their strict rules, the novices were not allowed to speak, except when spoken to or asked a question.

Sister Barbara recalls that everyone had daily chores at the motherhouse in addition to their studies for teaching at Ursuline College. They were assigned to laundry, kitchen, setting and cleaning tables, sewing room and robery, and cleaning. Sister Barbara was good at sewing, so she was assigned to the sewing room and helped to sew numbers on everything that passed through the laundry that correlated with each person. She also did some cleaning chores.

One day during these early years, she was washing the stairway with her head down, scrubbing the steps and crying. Not being able to express herself in words, because of the rule of silence, she was feeling frustrated. She had been hoping to study and teach music but had been told that morning that music was not going to be part of her teaching degree.

A black veil, or professed sister, was walking up the stairs and saw her crying. She came over to her and whispered, "Don't worry, Barbara, God will keep your music safe in your heart."

Those few words of encouragement comforted the young Sister Barbara and she felt better. My sister has often told me that the kind words or actions from the other sisters, as she was traveling her religious journey, became the motivation that kept her going.

Another six months passed filled with discipline and more study. In the fall, the white veils would begin teaching the children in nearby parochial schools.

The new teachers would leave the motherhouse each morning on a school bus. They would be transported to their classrooms at different diocesan schools within a five-mile radius of the motherhouse. They were all directed to wear a black veil in public, even though they were still white veils, so as no attention would be brought upon them.

Sister Barbara's first assignment was Grade 2 at St. Jerome School in Cleveland.

After World War II, the population had swelled in the United States, affecting the numbers of school-age children across the country. Class sizes were usually large, sometimes 40 – 50 children. Establishing multiple grades began in earnest and the need for teachers became great.

I attended St. Jerome's when Sister Barbara was teaching and was placed in another second grade down the hall from her classroom. In fact, my teacher, Sister Theophane, was Sister Barbara's mentor and supervisor. I wasn't aware, nor were other people, that Sister Barbara was basically a student teacher still earning her degree. She recalls how, every once in a while, Sister Theophane would stand outside her classroom door and smile, a signal that she was doing a good job. If she appeared straight-faced, then something was wrong and needed to be corrected. I never noticed this routine, nor did anyone else. The two nuns did a good job of hiding any problems.

In fact, my brother and I, who was in fifth grade, hid things also. We were given strict instructions not to acknowledge Sister Barbara as our real sister. No one was to know we were related. Sometimes, after school and before our bus ride home, we would sneak a few furtive glances into her room and maybe give a wave on our way to the bus stop. Occasionally, she wanted to give us a hug but we had to wait until no one was around and even then, the door had to be closed. It felt strange but also exciting and a little mysterious.

By the end of the school year, in 1955, the whole school had eventually realized that we were related. Maybe it was because we resembled each other, or that my brother and I were always in her classroom, either before or after school. By the next fall term, Sister Barbara was transferred to St. Charles Parish in Parma, a suburb of Cleveland, twenty miles away. She moved into the St. Charles Convent near the school and taught first grade.

Every Sunday, no matter what during those early years, my brother, my sisters and I would climb into the family's 1952 powder blue, four-door Dodge Coronet and drive with our parents to the Cleveland's West Side to visit Sister Barbara. It was a long ride, maybe forty-five minutes along the freeway, but also fun because we knew that on the way home, we'd stop for dinner. We would eat at Howard Johnson's or the family restaurant called Tick Tock on Brookpark Road. Our mother worked during the week so the last thing she wanted to do on a late Sunday afternoon was to cook.

In the summer of 1958, Sister Barbara moved again. She was assigned to St. Ann's Parish, ten miles closer to us in Cleveland to teach Grade 1. We visited every Sunday, but by now my older sisters were too busy with their own lives to come with us each week. My brother and I continued on these road trips but were now passengers in a yellow and white 1957 two-door Mercury Monterey. Very luxurious, and we never missed a chance to eat out on the way home.

*Whenever I heard that my family was having a party or getting together for a picnic, it would make me sad, as I could not come or go to their homes. My tears came, but I would pray for all of them to have a good time and asked God to take care of them. —S.M.B.*

Sister Barbara kept following her path to remain an Ursuline and to teach, even though there were multiple restrictions placed on her every day. It was their founder, Angela Merici, who continually inspired Sister Barbara and who helped her focus on her goal of serving the Lord.

*As time went on, I began to learn more about St. Angela Merici – the Foundress of our Ursuline Community. She lived during the Renaissance in Northern Italy, a contemporary of Christopher Columbus, Ignatius of Loyola, and Martin Luther. Angela believed that it was good to change according to the needs of the times, with prudence and good advice or common sense. She looked around and noticed that no one was caring for the women and children. She began gathering the women together for support and prayer, helping them to lead Christian lives in a decadent society – one much like our present culture of violence.*

*Originally, the women lived in their homes. In the 17ᵗʰ century the Church said, "Oh, no!" and put them into a convent. But we Ursulines were smart enough to say, "Oh, no!" and took a fourth vow of Education, enabling us to do social outreach. Angela was ahead of her times. It never occurred to her that she would not be able to do what she needed to do. —S.M.B.*

At St. Charles, there were several black veils but only three juniors at the convent, including Sister Barbara. The parish had purchased a new TV for the sisters. The juniors were not allowed to watch. One evening, everyone was sitting in the community parlor. Most were watching TV but the three juniors had their back to the TV screen.

A black veil turned to face them as they read in the corner and said, "Come on over here, you work just as hard as we do." From then on, all were included in the occasional relaxation of laughing at *I Love Lucy* or *Ozzie and Harriet*.

Sister Barbara reminded me that it was this kindness, once again, from so many sisters that helped her stay in the Ursulines so that she could pursue her ministry of serving the Lord and his children. She made her final vows in September 1958.

# CHAPTER FOUR

# VATICAN II

*I*n the fall of 1961, Sister Barbara returned to St. Jerome's as a first grade teacher. I saw my sister every day while in the eighth grade, my last year at St. Jerome's. My brother was already in high school and I was on my way to the upper grades at the local Catholic high school.

My mother was active in the Altar and Rosary Society, a women's group at the parish. Once a year they would hold a Mother and Daughter Celebration of Mass and a breakfast. My mother was in charge of the kitchen and, of course, I was there by her side to help in the setup and cleanup.

I remember one Sunday very well. The breakfast was over and the cleanup had begun. As I placed dirty dishes into the sink to be washed, I overheard my mother reprimanding a woman at the far corner of the large kitchen. "What are you doing?" she asked as a large spoon was yanked out of the woman's hand.

"I'm trying to gather the extra food for the poor sisters at the convent."

"Well, those are table scraps. You shouldn't be collecting food from people's plates." The whole bowl was dumped into the garbage.

The woman, being scolded, stared in disbelief.

My mother stood her ground. "No daughter of mine is going to eat table scraps like a dog."

Embarrassed as I was, I had to agree. Our mother was always a straight-laced soldier and advocate for her children, and that still included Sister Barbara, even though she was now under the care of the Ursulines. It didn't stop her from protecting her daughter.

A sense of pride came over me and a new respect for my mother grew as I walked across the parking lot to the convent carrying the shopping bag filled with untouched extra eggs, bacon, and sweet rolls. Coincidently, Sister Barbara answered the door, and after a couple of big hugs, I told my sister, "You wouldn't believe what Mom did now." The food was handed over with a quick explanation. She smiled, and I sensed that she knew the meaning of my words. No one messes with our mother when it comes to family.

To this day, as I volunteer at Church preparing food for shelters or the needy, I'm always careful and try to make sure the food presentation is just right.

Over the next several years, Sister Barbara remained at St. Jerome Parish teaching grade one. During that time, she attended classes every Saturday, eventually earning her Bachelor of Science in Education in 1962, and then continuing on to earn a master's degree. My parents were thrilled that she once again lived within the family neighborhood.

*******

The planning of the 21st Ecumenical Council in 1965, known as Vatican II, was daunting for the Church. Roman Catholic religious leaders from all over the world were called upon to discuss the future of the Catholic Church. There hadn't been an assembly of religious leaders tasked in settling doctrinal issues for 100 years. This assembly was not to handle a crisis, it was to discuss the cultural changes that were occurring after World War II and affecting the Church.

It was a long process to bring together 2000 – 2500 bishops, thousands of observers, auditors, sisters, laymen, and laywomen. There were four sessions scheduled during which 16 documents were formalized. The basic themes included: Reconciliation, permission for Catholics to pray with Christians, and encouragement of friendships with other non-Christian faiths. It opened the door for languages besides Latin to be used in the Mass.

Vatican II showed the Church's willingness to operate in the contemporary realm and shaped the modern Church of today.

The Ursulines began incorporating many of the principles from Vatican II. In 1968, Sister Barbara was asked if she would volunteer to go to El Salvador with a group of sisters who were establishing a mission in this small South American country.

*I volunteered to go to El Salvador to start the Cleveland Mission. The first two applicants agreed to go. I was third in line and planning to return to teaching in the fall, so I was not chosen. I was disappointed, but then received a call from Sister Marie deLourdes. She asked if I would be interested in ministering at a "mini El Salvador" on the near-west side of Cleveland. The Ursuline community agreed to send Sister Mary Dolors as Principal, and to merge two Catholic Schools, St. Patrick and St. Malachi, into one school. Other sisters were invited to join Sister Dolors. It was quite challenging and exciting. It is still operating today as Urban Community School. — S.M.B.*

This time, our parents were terrified that their daughter would be sent away to a dangerous situation and were relieved when she stayed in Cleveland.

Their fears were not unfounded. Several years later, in December 1980, one of the Ursuline sisters who had volunteered to minister to those at risk from violence and war in El Salvador was murdered.

"On the night of December 2, 1980, Sister Dorothy Kazel, Cleveland, lay missioner Jean Donovan, and Maryknoll Sisters Maura Clarke and Ita Ford were abducted from the La Libertad airport, interrogated, physically and sexually abused, and shot by five national guardsmen. The next morning they were found buried in a common, shallow grave, marked with a cross of two branches. On December 4, the women's bodies were drawn from the burial site. Dorothy's body was returned to Cleveland, Ohio, where Bishop Anthony M. Pilla celebrated the Mass of Christian burial at the Cathedral of St. John the Evangelist December 10, 1980."[1]

*The night Dorothy died, her mother woke up in the night with chest pains and woke up her husband. They did not know of her death until 24 hours later.*

*A phone call to Sister Martha Owen at St. Malachi convent, where I was living, informed us that Dorothy*

---

[1] Words taken from Ursuline Sisters of Cleveland website.

*was missing. All of us stood in the hall near the phone, knowing that she was probably dead.*

*A bus of Gilmore students was driving past the Ursuline Motherhouse the night Dorothy died. They stopped the bus to view the red aura in the sky that had enveloped all of the buildings on the Motherhouse property.*

*The* Cleveland Plain Dealer *published a lot of untruths regarding this event. That's when I began to be more watchful over reported news on TV, radio and in newspapers.  —S.M.B.*

# CHAPTER FIVE

# SISTERS

*"Saint Angela Merici teaches us to go with what is
needed and change."* —S.M.B.

The Ursulines, including Sister Barbara,
continued to wear their black habits and to
follow several strict restrictions governing their
lives, even though Vatican II began to ease some of
the laws of the Church.

When our sister, Ann, was married to Tony in
1967, at St. Jerome Parish, Sister Barbara was living
in the convent and teaching at the school.

*I was unable to attend my sister's wedding ceremony
as it was prohibited by my rule. But I figured out a way
to be there. My job as sacristan often kept me in the
sacristy, a small room that was next to the front altar, all
Saturday. As I sewed or mended altar linens, I was able*

*to watch the wedding ceremony through the open doorway. After the ceremony, they both came to where I was standing and I congratulated both of them with a big hug. A few weeks later, Ann told me that Tony was flustered by my hug and kiss, as he had never been kissed by a nun! — S.M.B.*

Sister Barbara became an assistant principal in 1969, earning her Master's Degree in Education and Montessori training a year later. In this administrative role, she taught Grade 1 and co-directed the merger of three parish schools (St. Malachi, St. Patrick, and St. Wendelin) into the Urban Community School, which served the economically poor in the near-west side of Cleveland.

My husband and I were married in that busy year of 1969. Ours was a traditional Catholic service, except that we had a few things we wanted to do that no one had ever done before. Armed with Vatican II behind our requests, we asked for a guitar Mass and to sit in the sanctuary within the altar area near the priest so we could face the congregation as we were introduced as Mr. and Mrs. Timothy Struna. The parish priest granted us our wishes. Sister Barbara enlisted a seminarian friend to assist her in the music and liturgical songs. Many pictures were taken at the wedding and to this day, my children are always amazed at Sister Barbara's clothes as they flip through the pages of our wedding album. At that time, she still wore the long black robe but the starched wimple around her face was gone, replaced with a smaller veil. Soon, her habit would go through a bigger change.

While she was living at St. Patrick-Malachi's, an event occurred that she still laughs at today. As religious sisters across the country instituted changes suggested by Vatican II, the Ursulines were not to be excluded.

*We dressed in black habits from head to toe. We scared a lot of children.* —S.M.B.

In the spring of 1970, Sister Barbara was asked to sew samples of a new habit and model them to the hierarchy. After much discussion and several pattern designs, the dresses awaited final approval.

One winter Saturday morning in the early seventies, before the young sisters left for their college classes and workshops at St. John College, word came down to them that they would be allowed to wear their new habits. The new habits consisted of a grey mid-length dress and a small veil. Gone were the black robes and starchy wimples. The sisters quickly changed into their new outfits. They then proceeded, as a group, to go behind the convent and throw their traditional uncomfortable garments into a huge metal barrel, and light them on fire. Standing around the burning clothes, they all laughed. It was liberating. After several expressions of joy and, "Thank you, Jesus," they left for their college classes.

Some nuns, who did not like the changes and were frightened by them, continued to wear the black habits.

*I was never afraid. I accepted the changes and moved forward. My independence kept me strong in my decisions to do things a certain way, in order to teach children so they could learn. If I met someone with an idea that I did not like, I would not get angry or frustrated, I would say in my heart, "I will never do that." Then as I passed them, I kept smiling and pretended as if I had agreed to what they said.* —S.M.B.

"There is only one way to turn every ending into a fresh beginning. That is to make a friend of change. By doing so, we're able to let go of the familiar and move on, bringing our full attention to whatever comes next."

—*The Time of Your Life: Reflections on Growing Older*, Herb and Mary Montgomery

As many women's religious orders continued to change, the sisters grew more independent. Those who didn't have their license learned to drive; some balanced a checkbook for the first time.

In the summer of 1973, a little incident brought home the fact that Sister Barbara, because of her cloistered life, had a lot to learn about finances. My mother had invited all of us to go on a family vacation, including Sister Barbara. A nearby state park in Ohio had cabins to rent so we all decided to gather for a week in the woods. Sister Barbara took up residence with our parents. The week before, my mother had taken her shopping for a bathing suit, Bermuda shorts, and appropriate clothing for a summer of fun.

One day, mid-week, each family had chosen to do an independent activity. My husband and I decided to stay at the cabin to make sure our young boys would get their naps, along with a nap for both of us. I was a stay-at-home mom and my husband was a teacher. With one income, we didn't have a lot of expendable money.

Sister Barbara chose to remain behind with us that day, explaining that some of her sister friends were coming to visit. She wanted to provide a nice picnic lunch for them and asked if we could give her some money to go to the store to buy food for their lunch. We only had a $50-dollar bill but gave it to her anyway, hoping for change when she returned. That was not the case. She spent it all and we were left with no cash for the rest of the week. We laugh about it now, but we were nervous at the time.

Thank goodness for Vatican II because as the years went by, she and all the sisters were given many more opportunities to learn about finance, and eventually all became successful businesswomen in matters of administering the affairs for their ministries. In fact, Sister Barbara, over her career as administrator of several schools, raised and managed over $1,000,000.

**Letter to our mother** – written by *S.M.B.*

*Dear Mom,*

*Among all the things you taught me, "Honesty is the best policy" is high on the list. Remember when I was about seven or eight years old and I decided to sell popcorn balls, like Francy and Dorothy, who attended public school? It didn't matter to me that my school did not have this fundraiser. I very carefully made order blanks on a small tablet and walked from door-to-door (only to the houses between the lamp posts, of course) asking people to order popcorn balls. Most of the people paid in advance.*

*Thinking you would never find out, I sat on the front porch, close to the wall, counting the money and checking the orders. You heard the noise of the money and came out to ask me to explain what I was doing with so much money, (mostly pennies and nickels).*

*You then stopped your work and gathered up Pat and Anna Mae and marched me to each house that had ordered popcorn balls. While you stood at the street, I had to walk up the sidewalk, by myself, to the door, ring the doorbell or knock, and explain what I had done. Then I had to return the money.*

*Most of the people took one look at my mother and knew I was in trouble. They very kindly told me that I could keep the money but I insisted that they had to take it. I did not have to look at my mother to know that they had better take the money. This took a long time.*

*You may remember more details, but I know the awful feeling inside me while I was returning the money. I promised myself at this very young age that, "Honesty is the best policy."*

*Thank you for helping me learn the hard way, but of course the best way.*

*With lots of love,*

*Sister Barbara*

# CHAPTER SIX

# VACATIONS

*I*n the early '70s, and years after Sister Barbara took her final vows, new rules enabled her to finally visit us at home for holidays, go on a vacation, or go out to a restaurant. Yes, I said, vacations, and Sister Barbara loved to travel.

*Some places I remember as a small child.*

* *Geneva On The Lake, in Ohio with the Eppich and Pawali Families – We were rolling down a small hill near the barn. Someone hit a bees' nest in the grass. I was stung all over my body. Mom put cold compresses on me as I lay in the back of the car all the way home. Thank God I was not allergic to bee stings. Age 10.*

* *Avon Lake, Ohio and the Eppich and Herbst Families*

★ *Metropolitan Park, Cleveland, Ohio and the Gron Family — at this park all the grownups played baseball and included the children, too.*

★ *-Snake Rock, Ohio*

★ *-Niagara Falls, 1948. We always stopped to see the falls on the way to New York or Chicago to visit relatives. Once, Aunt Alice and Uncle Bill Eppich invited me to come with them to Niagara Falls to help take care of their children Patty, Billy, and Linda. It was my eighth-grade graduation gift.*

Uncle Vic and Aunt Allie Lou Moisio lived in Mentor, Ohio, in a small house. Uncle Vic owned his own business. We often went there in the summer for swimming. I thought Uncle Vic was handsome and lots of fun, always joking. Mom covered her arms and legs when sitting in the sun on the beach. She often made a tent out of sticks and towels. She was a good swimmer and, as she grew older, her skin never looked wrinkled.

I knew Vic Moisio as 'Uncle Vic.' Actually, he had been Mom's boyfriend. After Dad married Mom, Vic met Allie Lou and married her. All four remained good friends.

While in high school, 1950, I vacationed in Upstate New York with my best friend, Lucienne O'Keefe, and her family. We took a walk down the street and stopped by the river. A young man was sitting on the ground by a tree. I stopped. He looked at me and smiled.

*It was such a beautiful place; it made me cry ever so softly. He asked if something was wrong. I said no, it was just such a beautiful place, and then Lucienne and I walked home.*

*The next evening, we took another walk into the countryside. It was twilight. We walked to the top of a hill and looked down into the valley. The mist was rising, and in it were millions of fireflies, all lighting up the night and moving around. It was breathtaking – a light in the darkness! As the sun continued to set, the sky became a beautiful color. We sat down on the side of the road in silence.*

*The beauty of nature – thank You, God.  —S.M.B.*

As I grew older, we celebrated many of my late-June birthdays at the same Geneva on The Lake cottage. The once-a-year family reunions at Metro Parks Welch Woods continued without Sister Barbara. These multi-family picnics were always such fun. No matter your age, you'd become a member of either family's baseball team and, with patience and encouragement, would be able to score a run or a hit.

In the late '50s, my mother would continue outings to Metro Park on warm spring or summer evenings. She would prepare a picnic supper and then we'd all wait for Dad to come home from work. Mom never learned to drive, so we needed him.

Many times, he was tired, but he still agreed to go on the picnics with us. I admired the spontaneity of my mother for adventure, and our Dad's love for us in consenting to go to the park. Today, I still look forward to spur-of-the-moment outings with my own children.

*In 1974, I made a trip on the* William G. Mather, *an iron ore ship docked in Cleveland, Ohio. I was invited with six other Ursuline sisters from Urban Community School to sail on the* Mather. *Father Paul Hritz gave us the Blessed Sacrament to take with us for communion services. It was in a black box inside a black bag and placed in my black suitcase. I stowed it under my bed for safekeeping. Each day, we gathered together for a communion service while on board for the eight days of travel.*

*One night, as we entered Lake Huron, a storm came up, a gale with 25 to 30 mile-per-hour winds. The Captain anchored the ship near the shore. He told us to secure to the walls all beds, dressers, and chairs using the hooks on the furniture, then to get into bed.*

*We were rocked to sleep. The next morning, he told us that he actually had dropped anchor until the storm ended. Then on the way to Lake Superior and going through Sault Ste. Marie, a very thick fog came upon us. You could hardly see your hand in front of your face. Once again, the Captain told us to stay in our cabins and go to sleep. The next morning, he ate breakfast with us. He told us that as the ship was moving through the locks, he could almost touch the ship in front of the Mather.*

*He said, 'It was a miracle we didn't hit!'*

*We said, 'It was the Blessed Sacrament!' We then informed him of the presence of the Eucharist on board, in the bow of the ship. We all agreed that it was certainly a miracle or two! —S.M.B.*

In the late '70s, Sister Barbara would occasionally accompany our parents on their annual spring trips to Florida. Prior to these outings, Mom would take Sister Barbara shopping for new summer clothes, including a bathing suit. We often laughed about what her little students would say if they knew she went swimming.

In 1981, she flew to meet our parents in Port St. Lucie. Dad was beginning to feel sickly and Sister Barbara was going to be their chauffeur. Many of Sister Barbara's trips demonstrated her physical stamina and determination.

*March 19, 1981. Dad was not feeling well. Left Cleveland at 7 a.m. in heavy snow and 23 degrees. Arrived West Palm Beach at 1:25 a.m. cloudy, cool and 25 mph winds. Rented a car and drove to Mom and Dad, arriving at 4:30 p.m. – up almost 24 hours. Took a walk with Dad, went to bed early. Enjoyed walking, beachcombing, swimming, visiting with Mom and Dad, and relaxing until March 23. I left at 5:15 p.m. for chilly Cleveland, Ohio. Tim and Barbara flew in to help drive Mom and Dad home. —S.M.B*

In late June 1988, my husband and I moved our three teenagers to Cape Cod to start a new life on the East Coast and further his career as an artist. We sold our house, business, and commercial building. No surprise to us, it became an organized chaos. Sister Barbara, in early July, was our first overnight visitor. She stayed for two weeks.

When she arrived, most of our belongings were still in boxes and the old 1880 house was under renovation, with contractors and workers on site almost every day and in every part of the house. We'd made sure her bedroom was finished and the kids were comfortable. Our new bedroom was under construction, so we slept on an air mattress and stored our dressers and clothes in the barn.

Sister Barbara pitched in when there was a need and tried to suggest better ways of doing things. For example, trips to the store occurred daily, sometimes twice a day. Her suggestion was to "Make a list." Yes, she was correct, if I could only find paper and a pencil. We laugh about it now, but at the time, that was the last thing I wanted to hear in the midst of the madness.

She did bring with her a relative calmness and the familiarity of home, and for that, we are forever grateful. She has often told us that her visits on Cape Cod were akin to her going on a retreat, filled with peace, beauty, reflection, and fun. Her feelings reassured us that we'd made the right choice of leaving Ohio and starting over, at forty years of age.

*Cape Cod 1997: peaceful, songs of birds, gardens full of roses, herbs, time to read, time to walk, time to think, breathing. Porches large and small, chairs and rockers, a colorful trellis, and shades of green, dark and light.*

*—S.M.B.*

In 2000, Sister Barbara had flown Northwest Airlines to Cape Cod for her annual visit and the wedding of our niece, Kristen Eppich, to David DeMuth.

*Left for the airport at 8:30 a.m. to check in leisurely. No trouble at desk. Went to gate and sat quietly reading a book. At 10:00 a.m. it was time to board but no one called our flight.*

*At 10:15 a.m., there was an announcement that they were fixing a navigational part and we were expected to leave at 10:30 a.m. We boarded at 10:45 a.m. and then proceeded to exit the plane at 11:00 a.m. because the part would take too long to repair. Our flight was then cancelled.*

*Waited in line for a new flight at noon. Now we were flying to Detroit! At 12:30 p.m. we boarded for Detroit with a ten-minute delay due to rainstorms. Finally, the plane was cleared for take-off at 1:05; we left at 1:30 p.m.*

*Arrived in Detroit at 2:30 p.m. and was told to go to Northwest and get another ticket to Boston. The earliest flight was at 11:30 p.m.! The attendants suggested a 9:00 p.m. flight to Providence, R.I. or maybe check other planes and be on 'stand-by.' All flights to Boston were delayed or cancelled due to weather.*

*Ate a good meal at 3 p.m., walked around to check other flights. At 5 p.m. the Detroit airport closed due to electrical storms. Around 7 p.m., the skies brightened and the planes began to finally fly in and out. Flight to Providence remained at 9:00 p.m. I kept trying to find a quiet place to sit. After several gate changes, Providence, R.I. was my ticket to Cape Cod. Looked for a phone to call Barb and Tim, there were no cell phones. Northwest gave me a six-minute calling card and $5.00 certificate for food and a ticket reduction. We boarded at 9:30 p.m., left at 10:00 p.m. and arrived in Providence at midnight. Tim picked me up at 12:45 a.m. and made it to Brewster at 2:45 a.m. Oh my, what a ride!*

*It was a beautiful wedding even though the weather was cool and rainy. My flight home repeated the same pattern of delayed and cancelled flights. I understand why some people call Northwest Airlines…Northworst!*

*—S.M.B.*

Each Cape Cod vacation that Sister Barbara embarked on was a unique experience. From traveling in the airports and on the old roads and quaint streets of Cape Cod and the Islands, to meeting new people and friends, she always learned something new or shared bits of her wisdom.

*Three weeks on Cape Cod! Time to unwind, relax. I read two books, saw a marching band in Orleans, shopped in Chatham, Orleans, Wellfleet, went to the Dennis Lighthouse Restaurant. Went to the beach everyday to touch the sand. I was able to get to church several times. We saw* Pirates of the Caribbean *and I began to read* Harry Potter. *I finished two puzzles.* —S.M.B.


*June 2007 to Cape Cod from Cleveland, Ohio*

*Cleared through security, I walked to Gate 22. Ate a fruit cup, oatmeal-raisin cookie, drank water. Stopped at the bathroom and walked back to Gate 22. The plane was ready to depart. My seat was at window 10A.*

*When I arrived at my seat, an elderly gentleman and lady smiled and said, "We've been waiting for you." It took them a while to get up and stand in the aisle so that I could sit down. I threw my bag over the seats. The gentleman said, 'Good throw!' I replied, 'I direct a preschool.' They both laughed and then we had a pleasant conversation.*

*As I left the plane, I thanked the stewardess and told her to tell the pilots they did a good job. She said, 'You tell them.' So I did. As I stepped close to the cockpit, I said, 'I always pray for the pilots and workers when I travel.'*

*They laughed and thanked me for my prayers. I stopped to buy crackers and complimented the clerk on his smile. I told him that my preschool children cannot come to school without a smile. He laughed.* —S.M.B.


Wherever you traveled with Sister Barbara, she would stop and tell her story to anyone whom she came in contact with. It made a slow pace for those traveling with her, always waiting until she finally said goodbye to complete strangers. During her many visits on Cape Cod, it was hard to accept this little habit of talking to whomever she met.

Her method of greeting always began with a compliment for the clerk, waitress, or the person standing in line with her, and then, a recap of, "…I'm an Ursuline sister and a pre-school teacher for inner city kids and…" Most often, a whole new conversation would begin and the two strangers, now friends for the moment, would talk with her for a few minutes and end with a goodbye and a laugh or a smile and a "God bless you" from Sister Barbara.

*I am always surprised with the harmony that God gives to us as we walk among the people each day. I try to remember to smile and look into the other's eyes. Slowing down helps one to be more friendly. Treating one another with respect is a way to be a healing presence. One must first be a safe place within in order to create safe places wherever you go. O God, give me an understanding heart.*
*—S.M.B.*

I was never aware of her causing harm or angering anyone. Her practice of saying a longer hello than normal was probably only a distraction for me, or those who were with her at the time. I remember I was usually in a hurry, minding the kids, trying to complete errands in a timely manner, or just uncomfortable in the summer heat and wanting to go home. Looking back, I regret that I didn't realize how important these little moments of kindness were and that this was part of her ministry of sharing God's goodness.

*To be happy is a gift to share. "Share your smile" means you have to have one to give. To share happy things, you have to be happy! So...just do it! —S.M.B.*

Sometimes Sister Barbara was rewarded with little gifts that just seemed to appear.

*June 2007 Cape Cod: Many families walk in the rain on Cape Cod, going in and out of stores just looking or trying to dry off. As I walk in my red raincoat, carrying my purse in the red bag that is made of the same material as the raincoat, and popping the red umbrella up and closing it down, I smile and step aside, careful not to poke anyone in the eye. I wonder who the people are; some speak a foreign language.*

*It's too far to walk to the beach, so I take short walks and return to Struna Galleries to rest. My niece, Barbara's daughter, Heather, owns the Struna Galleries in Chatham. Barbara and I try to visit Chatham at least once during my annual stays to give Heather a few hours to do some errands.*

*While Barbara watches the gallery, I walk and visit the Main Street shops. At the Mermaid's store, I bought a fairy princess and a pirate book in the children's section.*

*I saw another room and decided to walk in. Always looking at the floor to see where I'm going, I noticed a folded piece of paper. It was a $50-dollar bill!*

*I went to the register; excused myself and asked a couple if they lost any money. I said, 'I'm an honest lady. Did you lose this $50?' They said 'No.' I looked at the owner of the store, she shook her head and said, 'I guess you can keep it!' What a surprise. —S.M.B.*

The effects of her interesting life appeared occasionally during her travels. In the mid-'90s, a former student of Sister Barbara's, Rick Porrello, contacted her to ask if she could remember someone she grew up with. He was in the middle of writing a novel about the Irish Mafia in Cleveland, and the mobster Danny Greene was from Cleveland. Danny had attended St. Jerome's school at the same time she did.

*I knew Danny Greene, the Irishman, before he was a gangster. We attended St. Jerome Elementary School in the 40s. The school was taught by the Ursuline Sisters of Cleveland. In those days, boys and girls were separated. The boys were in one room and the girls in another, beginning in the sixth grade. Outdoor recess was also segregated; boys in the backyard and girls in the front yard. At dismissal, there were no buses or cars, only walkers. The east side stood by the left door and the west side by the west door. No talking, just walking.*

*Danny was the best boxer and baseball player. The priest in charge of athletes, Father Peter, told the boys that if they wanted to play on the team, they had to go to church on Sunday... so Danny did.  —S.M.B.*

She remembered him well and the book was published a few years later, *To Kill the Irishman: The War That Crippled the Mafia*. This led her to being interviewed in 2008 as part of the special features on the DVD for the movie, *Kill the Irishman*, inspired by Porrello's book. She was in the movies!

*Travelling to Cape Cod June 2015: I waited an hour on the plane. The pilot said, "We can't talk to Cleveland airport as the wire that connects us is not working. The mechanic tried to fix it and could not repair it." We had to board another plane. I met many people during this waiting period. Mr. Smith, a policeman at the Cleveland airport, recognized me as the "movie star" in* "Kill The Irishman." *He was a parishioner at St. Malachi Church and remembered when Danny Greene blew up Shondar Burns in the parking lot of St. Malachi's on Holy Saturday night; this scene was in the movie.*

*After landing, I boarded the bus to Hyannis. Very crowded. I took my purse off the aisle seat and held it in my arms. A tall man sat down holding his hat, coat, and bag. He was very quiet. Traffic going to Boston was terrific.*

*I looked across the aisle and said, 'Wow, I'm glad we are going in the other direction.' He smiled and said, 'I am an artist. It's always this way. I come to Boston on Monday and Tuesday to Art Class. My mother has Alzheimer's and I take care of her. My brother lives next door and he takes care of her when I'm gone. We live in Plymouth. My mother is 87 years old.'*

*I told him, 'I am 81 years old and coming to visit my family in Brewster. My sister is a published author and her husband is an artist.' He was quiet again. Then he said, 'My mother is beginning to forget who I am.' I thanked him for caring for his mother and agreed to pray for him and his family. —S.M.B.*

# CHAPTER SEVEN

# TEACHING

*T*he economic outlook for Cleveland, Ohio, in the late '70s was bleak. The city's government was in default and had over $15 million in debt. The population declined as businesses relocated outside of Cleveland. Property values decreased, which contributed to fewer property taxes collected and inner cities becoming poorer and run down. Churches began to consolidate and schools merged to keep a presence in these depressed neighborhoods.

The newly formed Urban Community School began to thrive under principal Sister Veronica Smerker and Sister Barbara as assistant principal. Sister Barbara also taught the preschool.

One of the key elements of Sister Barbara's teaching and administrative philosophy was compassion, respect, and discipline for all.

*I walked around the neighborhood and became friends with the parents. As time passed, the parents were more willing to come to school meetings and the students also wanted to be on time and liked to finish their assignments.*
                                                    *—S.M.B.*

Her unique style of promoting fellowship contributed to an increase in attendance and added to Urban Community's reputation for quality, which now attracted students outside of their district.

*In 1981, Sister Eugene, our Education Director, asked me how I liked Urban Community. I said, "I loved it." She then asked me how I would feel if I was asked to work somewhere else. I said, "I guess I would go."*

*The next week, I received a phone call telling me that I was needed to be a principal at Immaculate Conception School. —S.M.B.*

In 1981, when Sister Barbara left Urban Community School and was re-assigned to Immaculate Conception, students and parents shared their feelings as they said goodbye to her.

**STUDENTS**
Thank you for helping me when I was hurt in the lunchroom and on the school bus.

I wish you would not leave Urban Community. It's going to be boring without you. I hope they treat you nice at that new school.

Thank you for everything, like taking care of us when we are hurt, riding the bus, stopping fights, and ice cream treats.

Thank you for playing guitar and singing for us. I think you're number #1. I love you.

You are a sweet sister. You took good care of us, and the whole school.

## PARENTS

The things you gave were gifts from the heart.

Your sense of humor has saved many a day.

You have been a part of my and my children's life for ten years. I am glad we all got to know you. It's almost like a tradition. Thank you for teaching us the importance of quiet times.

You and your co-workers at Urban Community School have affected the lives of more families and individual people than any of the political and social programs which have touched base on the near West side. You have been at the heart of all things that have helped us be better people.

You were the first person to welcome us to your school. A place that is more than just a building; it's a family and a community. Something we now feel a part of, something that is part of you.

I know that you loved me. You helped me in my battle to be a good mother. You always had a smile on your face even when at times I knew you should not have the patience.

To a lady that I have always admired and loved. Thank you for all the times you sat down with me and listened to my problems and gave me advice.

You helped create Urban Community School with high standards, quality education and sincere love and concern for each child. USC has become the heart of the neighborhood. We hope other teachers will follow your example.

Immaculate Conception became Sister Barbara's work from 1981 – 1988. She taught third grade for one year and then became principal. Students, teachers, and parents loved her.

Her role during these years, besides teaching, was educating the parents through parent workshops and classes.

Her words hold true today.

*Children watch us (adults), our reactions to pressures, frustrations, authority, and daily living.*

*A child becomes what significant people in his or her environment tell him or her what he or she is. You are as others tell you.*

*Parents use the words punishment and discipline interchangeably, but there is a world of difference between the two. Punishment attempts to control people by some kind of force with the parent assuming the responsibility. Discipline is an active teaching process, which at its best helps children figure out how to cope with difficulties and places the burden of responsibility on the shoulders of the child, where it belongs.*

*Effective discipline is empowered with involvement. "I care about you and because I do, I am here to help you figure out a better way to behave."* —S.M.B.

As Sister Barbara continued in her ministry, she kept these observations from a few wise men in her heart and decided that dealing with children at any age has never been easy.

"We live in a decaying age. Young people no longer respect their parents. They are rude and impatient. They inhabit taverns and have no self-control."[2]

"The children now love luxury. They have bad manners, contempt for authority; they show disrespect for their elders. They no longer rise when elders enter the room. They contradict their parents, chatter before company, gobble up food at the table, and are tyrants at school."[3]

---

[2] *Inscription found on a 6,000-year-old Egyptian tomb*

[3] *Socrates, 5th century, B.C. Athens*

It wasn't until 1989 that her skills as an educator and administrator blossomed.

*In September of 1989, I was invited to be a part of merging another three schools, Our Lady of Peace, St. Benedict, and St. Catherine. My role was to turn a building at Our Lady of Peace into an Early Childhood Program for the three schools. In January 1990, the parish council of Our Lady of Peace decided to drop out of the merger.*

*I was teaching kindergarten at the time, and Sister Michael Marie, the principal, and I decided not to return for the next year. At a Martin Luther King celebration in February, I was asked if I would come to St. Joseph Collinwood and begin a preschool in their empty church space. The Ursuline community left Our Lady of Peace in June 1990, and I said yes to the preschool project at St. Joseph Collinwood in September. — S.M.B.*

Never wanting to sit idle, Sister Barbara planned and researched sites and consulted experts for advice on her new mission, as she taught music to grades K-4 and computer lab K-6 at St. Ann School. After one year, a decision was made that with renovation of the now empty St. Joseph Church, a preschool would be located in the rear of the building in the old entrance/foyer.

## CHAPTER EIGHT

## SAINT JOSEPH COLLINWOOD

*Historically, the Cleveland Diocese sent missionaries to establish a parish and school in the Collinwood area in 1871. They asked the Ursulines, who lived at Villa Angela several miles away, to teach. They walked the first days back and forth carrying their lunch in a basket. Fast forward to 1990, only two Ursulines remain as teachers at St. Joseph. I was asked to start a pre-school in the back of the church. Fifteen years later, I am still here and I often ask, 'Why me, Oh Lord?'  — S.M.B. 2005*

*S*t. Joseph's Collinwood was founded to serve the immigrants who worked for the New York Central Railway, which was the main link between New York and Chicago. The families of St. Joseph's grew over the years to almost 1800 parishioners. Today, many still live in the old houses that were built in the early 1900s.

In the mid-1960s, the population started to change. With the closing of the railroad yard and the 46-acre General Motors Fisher Body Plant, the availability of blue-collar jobs in the neighborhood evaporated. By 1989, the parish declined to less than 100 Catholic families.

Sister Barbara was invited, in 1990, to fill a desperate need for a quality neighborhood preschool childcare program. She was asked to organize and secure funding for the project. Based on her extensive background in early childhood education, and the fact that our family was raised in Collinwood, Sister Barbara brought an understanding and genuine concern for the needs of its residents. It was a three-part program consisting of day care, preschool, and parent education.

From its beginning, ninety percent of St. Joseph's student body were non-Catholic and African-American. Her enthusiasm and training in the Montessori method, which was originally created to help children from low socioeconomic backgrounds, was especially adaptable to the children in the school.

Soon, with an average of 22-26 students each school year, and aided with over $200,000 that Sister Barbara had personally raised through grants and donations, its name changed to St. Joseph Family Care Preschool. Guidance was given to mothers in obtaining state vouchers for their children.

Some parents qualified for scholarships or tuition assistance, or they would pay half and then volunteer for two hours per week. If that weren't possible, aunts or grandmothers would take the parents' places. The program also employed four women who, together with Sister Barbara, saw that the preschool ran smoothly in addition to offering before and after school care from 7:30 a.m. to 6:00 p.m.

During a workshop given to religious principals and administrators working at the time in Cleveland's inner city, Archbishop Lyke, the first African American bishop in Cleveland, reminded the sisters, "Remember, you may be wearing a veil but you are still a white woman, so when you drive around, lock your doors, close the windows, and put on the A/C…be careful."

Wherever I drove with Sister Barbara, she had a habit of locking her purse in the trunk so it would not be visible as she drove.

*The families of these children are very poor. Most of them are on welfare. When they feel they have some support, they do well. We do everything possible to involve the families.*

*I noticed that parents who helped out with classes also blossomed themselves during the school year. As they witnessed the value of their service, the change became visible in the way they dressed and carried themselves. This sense of pride was healthy for everyone involved in*

*the lives of these children. By how they act, children teach
me to love God, so I must act right for them to see me.*
*—S.M.B.*

As Sister Barbara was planning the details of the
school, a logo was needed, so she enlisted my
husband to design the essence of her school.

She had a few ideas, a love of nature and
especially trees, but nothing concrete. During her
summer visits with us on Cape Cod, we walked the
woods and beaches and talked, finally deciding on
the silhouette of an expansive oak tree. The words
Family Care Program surrounded leafy branches
atop three strong limbs of the tree. Tim added one
final touch of a swing to one of its boughs, a symbol
of Sister Barbara's teaching philosophy.

"The real joy of life is in its PLAY. Play is
anything we do for joy and the love of doing it, apart
from any profit, compulsion, or sense of duty. It is
the real living of life with the feeling of freedom and
self-expression. Play is the business of childhood
and its continuation in later years is the
prolongation of youth."[4]

*Children seem to be playing less and less these days.
We are taking away their childhood. We don't value play
in our society. Play deprivation can lead to depression,*

---

[4]*Walter Rauschenbusch - American theologian 1861-1918*

*hostility, and the loss of the things that make us human beings. We need to remember that play refreshes and stimulates the mind. It needs to take place in a safe environment and not be dominated by grown-ups. Hundreds of American elementary scholars have eliminated recess. Children need to learn how to navigate through life by themselves and keep their bodies safe.*

*The most important part of our culture is our particular family. What we learn about the world is determined by our experiences in the family and formed by our parents who create a unique world for us by their behavior.* — S.M.B.

The St. Joseph Family Care Preschool was able to give hundreds of inner-city children the social, cognitive, and academic skills needed to be successful in kindergarten. Family Care offered a safe environment to these children and promoted physical, mental, social, and spiritual growth. It provided a safety net for children who might be otherwise lost in a challenging district of the inner city.

The St. Joseph Family Care Preschool became the center of the Collinwood area and a loving part of the lives of all who passed through its doors.

*Parents, enjoy your children,*
*be in joy with them*
*look into their eyes*
*be with them.*
*Be relaxed with your children*
*Be unworried, be carefree*
*Have fun.*
*Don't be afraid*
*Of loving them too much,*
*Making mistakes with them,*
*Of being wrong,*
*Of apologizing.*
*Then your children*
*Will love you and you will love them*
*And love covers up our faults.*
*Amen*

—*S.M.B.*

# Photographs

*Maternal Grandparents Michael Gron married Rosa Gron in 1902*

*Gron Family Reunion 1954 - Welch Woods, Cleveland, Ohio*

*Paternal Grandparents with their three sons – 1942*
*Top Row standing: Carl, Pauline (Grandma Eppich, Tony (our Dad)*
*Second Row: William, Anton Sr. (Grandpa Eppich)*

*Dad (Anton Eppich) and Mom (Anna Gron)*

*Married 1932*

*Family Portrait 1952*
*Summer before Nancy left home to join the Ursulines.*

*Top Row: Dad Eppich; Nancy (Sister Barbara)*
*Middle Row: Barbara (myself), Mom Eppich; Michael;*
*Third Row: Patricia; Anna Mae.*

*Family vacation before Sister Barbara left for the convent*

*Sister Barbara's High School Portrait*

*Dressed and ready to say YES*

*Beginning a new life with the Ursulines at
Villa Angela, Cleveland, Ohio - 1952*

*Clothing Day - Becoming a White Veil (Novice) March 7, 1953*
*Nancy Rosemary Eppich was given a new name:*
*Sister Mary Barbara*

*Visiting Sister Barbara with my sisters, Patricia and Anna Mae*

*Visiting Sister Barbara as a family*

*Family visiting outside in the wooden folding chairs at Villa Angela;*
*I'm turned around in the front facing the camera.*

*After Sister Barbara took her final vows in 1958, she wore a black veil. Here are my sisters again. I'm in the front.*

*Dad and Mom with Sister Barbara*

*Visiting Sister Barbara at St. Charles Parish, Parma, Ohio in 1956*

*Mom Eppich and my sisters: Anna Mae, Barbara (myself),
Sister Barbara, Patricia*

*Sister Barbara in short veil*

*Sister Barbara visiting on Cape Cod*

*Sister Barbara playing with my youngest daughter, Anna,
on Cape Cod*

*Chatham Cape Cod*

*Provincetown Cape Cod*

*Sister Barbara teaching children St. Joseph Collinwood*

*St. Joseph Collinwood*

*Light of Hearts Villa with our brother Michael and me*

# Chapter Nine

# Difficult Days

As children who were raised Catholic, we were taught to respect the clergy beyond all else. In doing my research for this book, I discovered a list of clergy who were named in a database of Publicly Accused Priests in the U.S. The Cleveland Diocese listed 48 individuals. I dug further and found a priest with whom I had been familiar as a child. My brother had been an altar boy at the same time that this accused priest was at our parish school.

I remember my mother cautioning us to be careful around this particular person, especially my brother. He was not, under any circumstances to get into a car with him for an overnight retreat or even running errands. Our father would always drive our brother to the church and pick him up, even if it was inconvenient.

Our brother thankfully escaped any harm, but he remembers Mother's words of caution, thinking it was because she didn't want him to become a priest and lose another child to the church. I only recall the "stay away and be careful."

I'm forever grateful for my mother's keen instincts in protecting all of us.

The Cleveland diocese was pulled into the Sexual Abuse Scandals in 2002 after allegations of child sexual abuse at the hands of clergy were brought against the Archdiocese of Boston. Investigative reporting revealed several instances of years of abuse that were then covered up. Records from the 1950s and 1960s began to be released and priests were named, which brought a flood of lawsuits and financial troubles for the Catholic Church.

As far back as I can remember, the Church, and those involved, seemed to be in on the secrecy, from your neighbor to the local police. If something happened, it was reported locally but never went any further, especially if the police contact was a practicing Catholic. The Church's hierarchy took care of the matter in their own way, usually not believing the victim and sending the abuser to counseling, after which, these same priests would be allowed to continue in their parishes.

Many faithful Catholics lost their trust in the Church and left. Older churches, that were on the edge of closing due to financial obligations and now because of the lack of parishioners, began to close or consolidate. Money was needed to pay the courts and victims.

On July 21, 2005, Sister Barbara wrote to Bishop Anthony Pilla of the Cleveland Diocese (1981-2006). She had just returned from a retreat given by Joseph Nassal, CPPS. Father Joe specialized in retreats that featured renewal and reconciliation.

Over the years, via written letters, he became a dear friend and counselor of Sister Barbara. This time, she was so moved by her retreat with him that she was called to write this letter. In her ministry, Sister Barbara often uses praise or gratitude with discipline, as you will see in this letter to Bishop Pilla:

*Dear Bishop Pilla,*

*St. Angela told us to read the signs of the times, then act, have faith, make efforts, have hope, cry aloud. So...I decided to write to you.*

*While on my annual retreat at Villa Marie Retreat Center, I read the 'Plain Dealer' articles about your testifying concerning the sexual abuse problems in Cleveland. I brought you and our Church to prayer that day.*

*The theme of my retreat was 'Six Degrees of Reconciliation' given by Father Joseph Nassal, CPPS, whose mission in his Chicago community is reconciliation. I became familiar with his spirituality by reading one of his books, "Moments of Truth." I also attended his preached retreat at Our Lady of the Pines Retreat Center a few years ago. This week he spoke about being truth tellers and prophets.*

*The death of my sister Anna Mae Eppich Lang helped me to listen to her truth, as she died over three months. I am so grateful that you came to her home and offered her last liturgy with our family. Her great love for her faith, family, and friends spoke to all of us, even though she could not speak. I have asked my sister Anna Mae to watch over you on this painful journey. I know Tony, her husband, is supporting you also.*

*And I thank you for your support in my ministry to the Black African Community in Collinwood in the form of a preschool at Saint Joseph.*

*May the God who loves us with all our brokenness be with you in these trying days.*

*Sister Barbara Eppich. O.S.U.*

On May 1, 2008, a letter was delivered to three neighboring parishes from Bishop Lennon, Bishop of Cleveland, (2006 – 2016). He had replaced Bishop Pilla. It was the beginning of the end for Sister Barbara's school.

"This letter is to inform you that the Collinwood Schools Cluster, consisting of St. Jerome School on Lakeshore Boulevard, St. Mary School on Holmes Avenue, and St. Joseph School on Saint Clair Avenue in Collinwood have begun negotiations on consolidating their three schools into one school with possibly two campuses."

The atmosphere among the faithful Catholics and dedicated parishioners became filled with anger as long-standing churches were closed. Bishop Lennon, after being transferred from the Archdiocese of Boston to Cleveland, in May 2006, became the person who was sometimes admired and hated by local Catholics. He was put in a position that favored financial results, due to the sexual abuse scandals, rather than being a shepherd over 700,000 Catholics, and sadly, became best known only for the closing of 30 some churches in Northeast Ohio between 2008- 2010.

A few months later, these headlines appeared in the Cleveland papers:

**News Headline July 3, 2008.** "Former Chief Financial Officer of Catholic Diocese of Cleveland Convicted of Conspiracy and Filing False Tax Returns"

**News Headline July 8, 2008.** "A priest resigned from the Catholic Diocese of Cleveland after another allegation of sexual misconduct with a minor was reported."

It seemed to Sister Barbara, at 74 years old, that the Catholic Church as she knew it was under attack from within and beyond its confines.

She wrote another letter to Father Joe Nassal, CPPS on July 16, 2008:

> *Dear Joe,*
>
> *Some reflections after retreat as I walk through reality and the headlines in the Sunday papers.*
>
> *Drove to school to pick up mail, check answering machine and say hello to the summer campers. I was expecting a $2000 gift for my tuition scholarship program. When I opened the letter it was $4000. I cried and then I danced! Maybe God has other plans for Bishop Lennon's consolidation of schools?*
>
> *On another happy note, my new residence is indeed a safe place. The other sisters are real blessings. God usually gives us a safe place either in the place we live or within our ministry. So I shall try to listen and take courage and not be afraid. I've included a picture of Angela Merici as a dancer. The prayer reminds me of what you said*

*on retreat. I'm sure you saw the papers; the headlines reminded me of our conversation about TRUTH. Take care, be at peace, and continue to walk your talk, which is enveloped in truth with a listening heart.*

*I shall try to do the same.*

*S.M.B.*

Early May 2009 – *A decree from Caesar Augustus (Bishop Lennon) went forth that certain churches and schools were to close or merge. St. Joseph in Collinwood was on the list. —S.M.B.*

Within less than a year, in late May 2009, the Cleveland Catholic Diocese officially ordered The Saint Joseph Family Care Preschool to close after twenty years of providing a quality Pre-K program to hundreds of children. The administrators of St. Joseph School and Sister Barbara's Pre-K program never thought that their school would be the one closing, at least they had hoped the school would remain.

This decision would place Sister Barbara on a new journey. But where was she supposed to go to relocate her preschool?

*In our Ursuline community, we have always spoken of changing with the times, letting go of the past and moving on. But when it actually takes place, it is certainly scary. As I worked with children of families that were broken and breaking apart, I often wondered how long the Family Care Program at St. Joseph Collinwood would last. I purposely purchased a lot of movable things.*

*—S.M.B.*

**July 2009** - Letter sent to friends and family from Sister Barbara:

*As you may already know, the St. Joseph Collinwood Family Care Program became a casualty of the diocesan clustering process in June 2009. This Family Care Program, after 20 years of service, was forced to halt operations when Bishop Lennon closed St. Joseph Collinwood Elementary School.*

*After a month of prayerful and determined efforts on my part, Father Anthony Cassese, pastor of St. Jerome Parish, sent a letter to Bishop Lennon asking approval of the school's relocation, which was granted on July 28, 2009. The Diocese ordered that a lease be drawn up among the Ursuline Sisters, St. Jerome Parish, and the Cleveland Diocese.*

In several conversations with me during those months of waiting and wondering where her school would be located, I could sense the tension in Sister Barbara's voice and frustration in her not being heard. She told me of her meetings with Bishop

Lennon. At no time was she ever allowed to go into the Bishop's office, sit down and explain her school and the need for it in the community.

She would accompany Father Cassese to the meeting but never actually entered the Bishop's office; only Father Cassese was allowed into the meeting. The door was closed to her. She would remain outside the office, pace the hallway, pray, wait, and hold all the answers within that needed to be said to convince the Bishop that her school should be saved and relocated.

The relegating of women to a lesser degree of value has long been an acceptable method of treatment throughout the hierarchy of the Catholic Church. Even though men dominated major decisions and doctrine, there were always some priests who held a sincere respect for women. These men were the true shepherds, as they should be, and softened the exclusivity of others within the Church.

This pattern of behavior can be compared to the women's movement and its 'breaking the glass ceiling.' Sister Barbara had always been aware of this unequal partnership and yet, she remained on her journey as a sister in the Church. Dedication and her love of Christ kept her strong in her ministry. I believe she looked to the Church as a vehicle as she accomplished the good works in her heart.

Letter to Sister Ann Letitia Kostiha, October 2009:

> *...the St. Joseph building is all boarded up in white. I took pictures on Tuesday. The bishop has not said yes, yet, but maybe I am closer to my preschool being at St. Jerome. Grants are ready to go and estimates are in...but I am still waiting for GO. Mary of the Incarnation wrote: 'take care not to run before grace comes.'*
>
> *I am standing still....*
>
> *S.M.B.*

Letter to Joe Nassal, CPPC, December 1, 2009:

> *Dear Joe,*
>
> *My life is almost out of EXILE. I hope. Just began reading* Stations of the Crib – A Journey of Hope. *I often feel like the sign, "You are now beyond hope."*
>
> *I have often felt hopeless over these past months. And then something happens, a surprise or an unexpected event. My book is on hold but this chapter should be a best seller, not sure of title – maybe, "How to battle the bishop and WIN."*
>
> *I have been waiting several months for a lease. I called and sent faxes to the diocesan legal office even though they have told Father Casesse to tell me not to bother them. Also, I was never*

*invited to discuss the fate of the preschool. I was told Bishop Lennon no longer wanted to govern it. Thankfully, my Ursuline Community had a special 501-c-3 corporation and was able to take over the program, renaming it The Ursuline Child Care/Learning Center.*

*I will hopefully locate at St. Jerome Convent. Our lawyer, Sister Joanne, who also grew up at St. Jerome Parish, found a few problems in the lease (wrong name) and, also, they asked me to be responsible for the whole building's upkeep when I was only renting the first floor. This is what a landlord would do! I was told to let the lawyers work it out and so I, as the client, will remain silent and once again in EXILE.*

*Dorothy Day said: "No one has the right to sit down and feel hopeless. There is much work to be done."*

*So, I continue to wait in exile with an attitude of gratitude and trying to smile. I pray that I have the strength to take the risks that history demands of us.*

*S.M.B.*

# Chapter Ten

# Ursuline Family Care Program

*"If God takes you to it, he will take you through it."*
—*Sister Kendra Bottoms*

$\mathcal{A}$fter more than a year of negotiations and frustration, Sister Barbara was able to establish and open the Ursuline Family Care Program. Her original plan was to house the school in the now empty convent of St. Jerome's Parish but plans changed again.

Letter to Family and Friends, March 2010:

> *Dear Friends,*

> *Thank you for your prayers and support over the past eight months. With a grateful heart, I want you to know that the bishop signed the lease*

*for the St. Joseph Collinwood Family Care Program, a Montessori Pre-K Day Care of twenty years to begin again in St. Jerome Convent.*

*I hope to pick up the pieces to continue this much-needed ministry to children and families. The new name will be Ursuline Family Care Program. Construction will soon begin to prepare for a certificate of occupancy.*

*Sister Barbara*

Letter to Joe Nassal, CPPC:

*Dear Joe,*

*My faith, trust, and courage are all getting a 'work out.' My latest prayer is, 'Lord, heal my fears.' I am preparing a donor's mailing of 200 people who have helped me over the past twenty years. My brother owns a mailing business – so he will be able to do it for me 'pro bono.' Brothers Are Wonderful!*

*Sister Barbara*

After a summer of discussion with several contractors, a decision was made that the process of updating everything in the old convent to code would be too costly. But maybe there would be room for Sister Barbara to move her preschool inside the elementary school. More plans were drawn up and discussed again until finally, the Ursuline Family Care Program was ready to accept its new students.

Letter to Family and Friends, September 2010:

*My dear friends,*

*This thank you is to let you know that the Family Care Program is alive and well and housed in the annex of the St. Jerome's elementary school building. As of August 4, your combined donations of $18,346 to this ministry has made it possible to install a bathroom, enclose the coatroom for storage and a small office, and a new paint job, along with new carpeting.*

*The space will accommodate twenty children and, so far, fifteen have registered. On September 7, we will once again begin our full program of services. We plan to have an Open House in the fall to which you will be invited.*

*God's plan and time has brought this to new life. As the children, staff and I carefully re-create the twenty-year-old St. Joseph Family Care Program, I see God's wisdom everywhere lighting the way.*

*Thank you for your prayers, good advice, and contributions that made this miracle happen.*

*May God continue to give us the blessings of peace, good health and wisdom to be lights in the darkness of our world.*

*Gratefully, Sister Barbara*

"Ursuline Family Care Program offers preschool with convenience and history of success."[5]

On a visit to Sister Barbara in Ohio, she gave me a tour of the newly updated school facility. I entered the annex to the school and felt like I had been transported back to 1953 and to my first year of school.

It looked different, but at the same time, familiar. The old room had been repurposed into a Pre-K daycare. The cloakroom where we had hung our coats, hats, and book bags was gone, replaced by an enclosed office. Large windows still faced the playground; I remembered looking out and being a little nervous to run and play with new, and strange to me, children. My teacher, Miss Burke, was always kind but strict. There were probably fifty children in the class.

Sister Barbara handed me a mid-sized box. It was filled with over forty iron hooks that had lined the walls of the cloakroom. She wanted me to have them; I was flying home, so they would be shipped.

---

[5] *Collinwood Observer*, June 2011

We left the classroom so that I could meet the principal. I held onto the narrow wooden railing and walked up the dozen or so wide steps that led to a long tunnel-like hallway and into the main part of the school. I ran my fingertips along the smooth tiles that lined the walls, just like when I was little. It was fun walking down memory lane.

Weeks later, the heavy black hooks arrived on Cape Cod. I divided them up among my grown children, as a reminder of their Mom's schooldays and Sister Barbara's new schooldays at her relocated preschool. They now hold the coats, hats, and book bags of my grandchildren.

## CHAPTER ELEVEN

## LOVE OF DANCE AND MUSIC

*To me, life is like a dance. I create a dance wherever I go,
not always sure where I am going, but always trusting
and letting God take the lead.*

*—S.M.B.*

Prior to Sister Barbara opening the St. Joseph's Family Care Program in Collinwood for African-American children, she began to take aerobic dance exercise classes. She soon became a member of the Ohio and National Sacred Dance Guild and the St. Noel Dance Ministry. It was during this time in her teaching career that she incorporated her dance and music skills into the curriculum, including Praise Dancing, a form of liturgical or spiritual dancing focused on worship.

*I have prayed and danced all of my life but never felt
so complete as when I did them together. To express how
one feels is a gift. I DANCE to let my heart catch up with
my words. It gives me energy and direction.  —S.M.B.*

In 1994, the Vatican Congregation for the
Sacraments and Divine Worship issued *Dance in the
Liturgy* with new rules about dance liturgy. The
Vatican was not in favor of the dance liturgy.

"Among some peoples, singing is instinctively
accompanied by hand-clapping, rhythmic swaying,
and dance movements on the part of the
participants. Such forms of external expression can
have a place in the liturgical actions *of these peoples*
on condition that they are always the expression of
true *communal* prayer of adoration, praise, offering
and supplication, *and not simply a performance.*"[6]

Undaunted by stricter rules, Sister Barbara
continued with her dance ministry and began
offering workshops entitled, DANCING YOUR
JOURNEY: "Unless you become as little children…"

Her workshop was (described in *S.M.B.* words)
open to teachers, parents, grandparents, guardians
or anyone else who would like to enter a child's
world for a short time to gain some insights and
practical ideas to engage your children in

---

[6]Holy See's 1994 Instruction on authentic "inculturation"
of the Roman liturgy, *Varietates legitima*

meaningful play. Wear comfortable clothes; bring a SMILE, and a brown bag lunch.

In the brochure for the workshop, her bio was impressive:

> Sister Barbara is an Ursuline Sister presently directing and teaching at St. Joseph Family Care Program in Collinwood. She holds a bachelor's degree and a Master's Degree in Education, and is a certified Montessori teacher. Her added interest and training in music and liturgy led her to become actively involved in the music ministry of the many parishes she has served over the past 45 years as educator, administrator, musician, liturgist, song leader, choir member, and sacred dancer. She has choreographed solo dances and has conducted group prayer movements for retreats and workshops.

*In my life experience, I have found that my ministry serving the economically poor will succeed if it is God-centered. Our humanity is required to do the work but a healthy spirituality is a necessity. Along with my ministry of education I have always involved myself in the spiritual life of the parish as singer, musician, liturgical planner and dancer, encouraging those I meet to enhance their own creative spiritual destiny through music, dance, and art. The arts are very much a part of my spiritual journey.*

*Dance is a method of expressing our inward life with our outward expression. It is a response from the heart to God, a power of body and spirit working together in praise of God. The deepest purpose of the dance is to praise God and to give thanks. The silence of movement is like a wordless gentleness that flows out to all those present. It is as though the Holy Spirit is teaching us to pray using a new language. —S.M.B.*

Fast-forward to 2004: Francis Cardinal Arinze seemed to be at odds with Sister Barbara's words when he wrote, "Dance easily appeals to the senses and tends to call for approval, enjoyment, a desire for repetition, and a rewarding of the performers with the applause of the audience. Is this what we come to Mass to experience? Have we no theatres and parish halls, presuming that the dance in question is acceptable, which cannot be said of them all?"[7]

Even Pope Benedict the XVI, then Joseph Cardinal Ratzinger, wrote in *The Spirit of the Liturgy* (p.198): "It is totally absurd to try to make the liturgy 'attractive' by introducing dancing pantomimes (wherever possible performed by a professional dance troupe), which frequently (and rightly from

---

[7] *Celebrating the Eucharist* (p.53-54).

the professionals' point of view) end with applause."

Kathryn Mihelick in 2006, a member of the Sacred Dance Guild, prepared and submitted documentation for a definite ruling on Liturgical Sacred Dance to the United States Conference of Catholic Bishops, USCCB. They responded to Mihelick, telling her to submit to the Vatican for a decision.

A year later, they in turn replied that the decision remains with the USCCB. As of this printing, the USCCB still has refused to comment or decide the fate of Liturgical Sacred Dance within Divine Worship.

This was the climate that permeated the Catholic Church and yet, Sister Barbara persevered in her love of the dance and somehow stayed within the guidelines of the Church.

*In 2008, the Catholic Church seemed to be putting people back into the pews but my heart was still dancing.*
                                                              *—S.M.B.*

"When we are too self-conscious, we can't dance. Dancing frees the body and unleashes the spirit. By following the dance steps of Jesus, we are led out of ourselves and into God."

                                                   —Joe Nassal[8]

---

[8] *Conspiracy of Compassion*

*Life is constantly changing. Living is always a challenge and can be terrible or terrific depending on how you move through it. So why not choreograph a DANCE OF LIFE. It should be fun and creative. Use your imagination. Be Joyous and smile.* —S.M.B.

## CHAPTER TWELVE

## FRIENDSHIP

*My life as a religious woman is certainly different than it was in 1952, when I first entered the Ursuline Community. My call to ministry is still very challenging and fulfilling but my body is constantly reminding me that I have to conserve my energy and really only do one thing at a time and STOP before I do ONE MORE THING. —S.M.B.*

The number of American women choosing a religious vocation declined by 65% from 1965 to 2007. Many studies pointed to a growing trend of a weakened family life, especially Catholic families. The sexual abuse scandal and lack of trust in the hierarchy contributed, along with a declining birth rate in the United States.

Some religious felt they could do more in their ministry without all the restrictions placed on them by their individual orders or their Vatican superiors. Always sensitive to the signs of the times, the Ursulines adopted new rules and ways to foster more vocations. The sisters were encouraged to leave their communities and live closer to the people they served. Houses were rented or purchased by the Ursulines where three or four sisters would live together.

*Morning and Evening – Each day I begin and end in between. I meet many surprises and miracles in events and through people that are sent to me to touch with the divine living in me. O God, grant me wisdom and courage to be what you want me to be. Amen.* —S.M.B.

Even in the 1980s, the demise of religious vocations was evident to Sister Barbara and those around her. Letter to our sister Anne Lang's children, who were away at college:

*I am now sitting in the computer room at St. Ignatius High School. I have looked for your names on chairs, desks, etc., but can't find any memorabilia. I have spent two Saturdays learning about word processing on computers. It has been rewarding, as you can tell from this letter that took only ten minutes.*

*Each morning, I arrive at 8:30 a.m. and stumble up the stairs to the library. After a cup of coffee and a fresh donut, I take the elevator to the computer room. Both days were rather cold. At lunch, I enjoy looking out the window at the trees and flowers that are trying to grow around the campus.*

*I would like to inform all of you of another change in my exciting life as an Ursuline Nun of Cleveland. As you may have heard, religious life in general has been in the process of dying and rising in the past 10-20 years. Some communities have already died. Some are unable to continue due to lack of funds or lack of new life (members). Somehow, the Ursuline Nuns have been graced, (gifted), with the wisdom to die gracefully to those things that no longer apply to religious life in the 20th century and to dream together about the future. This 're-founding' of religious life is both exciting and frightening.*

*Don't panic… I am not getting married! I am being transferred, again, to another school. I also wanted to tell all of you that my expertise with young children has been enhanced by observing my nieces and nephews, especially the Lang family, as I spent so much time with you from your very early beginning.*

*May God bless you with a peacefulness that promotes good decisions as you move into your future. Don't forget to dream and for me, it's good not to forget to dance as it helps me to keep moving.*

*Love, Sister Barbara*

Letter to Family and Friends from Sister Barbara
  1994:

> *I have moved to a small house in Cleveland
> Heights with three other Ursulines.*
>
> *As the Cleveland Ursulines become smaller
> and smaller, older and, of course, wiser...we are
> being encouraged to choose to live in smaller
> community groups. In April of this year 1994, I
> was invited to join Sister Carol Pelegrin, a social
> worker at Metro Hospital, Sister Jean Iffarth, a
> Canon lawyer for the Cleveland Diocese, and
> Sister Ritamary Welsh, a council member of the
> Ursuline community, to rent a four-bedroom
> home from a young woman who volunteered for
> the Peace Corps as an English teacher in
> Hungary for two years.*
>
> *After two weeks of living together with only
> one bathroom, we are still at peace, building
> community, sharing our stories, attempting to be
> a blessing to one another, praying, laughing,
> working and visiting with those who drop in. We
> have called our home, 'Visitation House."*
>
> *For those of you unfamiliar with the Catholic
> Faith, the Visitation event is found in Luke's
> Gospel which describes how Mary, a teenager,
> journeyed to visit her much older cousin,
> Elizabeth, to share their common experience of
> pregnancy. So, we, too, see our home as a place of*

*greeting, support and friendship with all those*
*who journey to visit us.*

*S.M.B.*

June 2007
*...still an Ursuline sister after fifty-five years. Amen!*
—*S.M.B.*

With the growing uncertainty among religious women as to their future, the Church, in 2012, decided to investigate the good sisters across the country. In statements made by the Vatican's CDF, Congregation of the Doctrine of the Faith, some sisters were becoming 'radical feminists' and straying from doctrinal teachings, particularly the Leadership Conference of Women Religious, an association of the leaders of congregations of Catholic women religious in the United States. The conference represents nearly 80 percent of the approximately 48,500 women religious in the United States.

The statements from the Vatican were based on the groups' support of Obama's health care reform and the sister's excessive focus on poverty and economic injustice. The good sisters were also chastised for ignoring the directives from the Vatican to speak out against abortion and same-sex marriage and staying 'silent.'

At the same time of this initial reprimand, a widespread investigation of all the women's religious orders and communities was ordered, coupled with 'visitations' to each community.

I recall Sister Barbara's interpretation of the day that the emissary of the Bishop spoke to a large gathering of sister communities.

After listening to familiar words that have been heard before, with reserved respect on the part of sisters in attendance, tension began to rise among the women. Sister Barbara said she could feel it. She herself clenched her hands every time they were reprimanded and then preached ways to correct their errant behavior. Sadly, no questions were allowed, even though there were many.

## Excerpts from article written by Nicholas D. Kristof

"Catholic nuns are not the prissy traditionalists of caricature. No, nuns rock!

"They were the first feminists, earning PhDs or working as surgeons long before it was fashionable for women to hold jobs. As managers of hospitals, schools and complex bureaucracies, they were the first female C.E.O.s.

"They are also among the bravest, toughest, and most admirable people in the world. In my travels, I've seen heroic nuns defy warlords, pimps, and bandits. Even as bishops have disgraced the church by covering up the rape of children, nuns have redeemed it with their humble work on behalf of the neediest. So, Pope Benedict, all I can say is: You are crazy to mess with nuns.

'Since the papal crackdown on nuns, they have received an outpouring of support. Nuns were approached by Catholics at Sunday liturgies across the country with a simple question: 'What can we do to help?' The National Catholic Reporter recounted and cited one parish where a declaration of support for nuns from the pulpit drew loud applause, and another that was filled with shouts like, 'You go girl!'

"I'm betting on the nuns to win. After all, the sisters may be saintly, but they're also crafty. Elias Chacour, a prominent Palestinian archbishop in the Melkite Greek Catholic Church, recounts in a memoir that he once asked a convent if it could supply two nuns for a community literacy project. The mother superior said she would have to check with her bishop. 'The bishop was very clear in his refusal to allow two nuns,' the mother superior told him later. 'I cannot disobey him in that.' She added, 'I will send you three nuns!'"[9]

With the election of Pope Francis, in 2013, came a softening of the church's attitude toward religious

---

[9] Excerpts from an article written by Nicholas D. Kristof, *New York Times,* 28 April 2012.

women, which was started with the previous pope, Benedict XVI. Francis issued a statement in 2015. "When a consecrated woman is asked to perform a work of servitude, the life and dignity of that woman is demeaned," the pope said. "Her vocation is service: service to the Church. But not servitude!"[10]

*People are happy and good who found their vocation. What vocations there are, will depend upon the society within which they are practiced. We need to wake up and pay attention. —S.M.B.*

In April 2015, the standoff or investigation of the nuns ended. There had been so much of an uproar from parishioners across the country, protesting the treatment of the good sisters that everyone was relieved it was over. No doctrine was altered in this ending that affected the status of religious women but there was an inkling of hope that eventually, at some future time, their secondary status would be lifted and all would be equal. Change takes time and the sisters were willing to wait for their beloved Church to come to its senses.

*Historically, religious women have always met the needs of the time.*
*Our Ursuline community came to realize that each sister has certain gifts to use for the sake of their missions.*

---

[10] Pope Francis.

*By connecting to each other and with the laity, we are invited to collaborate by putting our gifts together to achieve new outcomes and share the power that it brings to us.*

*Collaboration became an important way to do ministry. It gave us new energy, life, direction, and hope within God's plan and in His time. We need to become the voice for the voiceless. We need to show up and be present, pay attention and then speak the truth, as we know it. Be open for outcomes. —S.M.B.*

There is a story from ancient history about the strength of women. Sister Barbara often retells the story of the Women of Weinsberg, Germany, in 1140, to whoever will listen.

A longtime ago, an army stood outside the walls of a city. The leader of the army shouted, "All women and children are free to leave the city before we ransack it. You have until dawn to decide what you will bring. You may take only what you can carry on your backs. At dawn you may leave and we will not harm you. Now I want to speak to your leader."

A beautiful woman appeared. He repeated to her, "Gather the women and children and whatever they can carry on their backs and be ready to leave the city at dawn." At dawn, the gates opened and out walked the children and the women were carrying their men on their backs.

# CHAPTER THIRTEEN

# SICKNESS AND DEATH

$\mathcal{S}$ickness is a part of life and death sometimes comes with it.

*Grandma Rose Gron – She came to live in our home on 1228 East 173rd Street when I entered the convent, in 1952. She was in her 70s but she had a bad heart (enlarged). In 1953, she became bedridden and began to sink into a coma. As a novice, I was not allowed to go home but since I lived three blocks from Villa Angela (The Motherhouse), I was told that I could visit my dying grandmother. Sister Louise Magyar would go with me.*

*Dad picked us up and when I entered the house, most of my uncles and aunts were crowded into our home. You could hear Grandma's breathing coming from the second floor. I went upstairs to say good-bye and give her a hug and a kiss.*

*Sister Louise offered to help my mother give Grandma Gron a bath. As I visited with my relatives downstairs, I found out that Sister Louise could speak Hungarian and came from the same village in Hungary that my grandmother left when she was eighteen years old to come to Cleveland, Ohio. What a surprise. Sr. Louise, who had nursing skills, was very helpful to my mother. Needless to say, Sr. Louise came to my grandmother's funeral and is probably one of the saints praying for me now.*

*—S.M.B.*

Death was not familiar to me when I was growing up; it had rarely shown its ugly face within our immediate family. I was lucky until 1976.

Our sister Patricia married Arnold Ruszkowski in 1960 and had three children. In February 1976, she died from a routine operation to remove plantar warts from her feet. She was thirty-eight, and their three children were all under thirteen years old. She was a wonderful mother and had already taught them kindness, respect, and to love each other forever.

I was living almost an hour away on our little farm in Montville, Ohio, when I got a call from my brother that I needed to get to the hospital as soon as I could. I had three young children under six and no second car. I waited until Tim came home from teaching and then we left for the hospital.

When we arrived, we were led to where Pat lay dying. Tim and I stood in the back to give her children a chance to say goodbye. There was nothing we could do but pray for those around her to find peace. I felt, because of all her pain, that Pat was already near God.

Years later, a court ruled in favor of her husband, Arnie, against the hospital and staff. The people who took care of Pat were found negligent in their treatment of his wife and our sister. Outdated and dangerous birth control medication over the years, combined with Pat's habit of smoking, had produced the terrible side effects of internal blood clotting. Her symptoms of severe pain and cramping were pushed aside by the doctors and nurses and labeled a mental condition. Sadly, this was not the correct diagnosis.

*My sister Patricia Ann died in 1976 from a simple foot operation. She was dead in three days. She left three children who are now married and have families of their own. Pat's husband, Arnie, remarried a widow, Felicia Vichill, who had four boys. Together they had seven teenagers! Wow! —S.M.B.*

Our father was next. August 1982.

*After surgery for a prostate gland, the anesthesia affected Dad's memory. He got worse at home. —S.M.B.*

I lived 45 minutes away from our parents and still only had one car, so phone calls became my way to keep in touch. I remember hearing over the phone the concern and worry in my mother's voice about our father. He was beginning to get angry with Mom and not remembering her or daily routines. He began to swat her away when she helped him in and out of bed.

She became anxious about her own strength and well-being. We all remembered our father as kind, understanding, and never violent to Mom or anyone else. His behavior seemed so strange to us.

She was determined to keep him home; after all, she was always the one in the family who took care of the sick and those needing help. Most importantly, this was her husband and she loved him.

After a close call of Dad pushing her and her almost falling, a decision was made to enter him into a clinic for a psychiatric evaluation. From there, he went to a nursing home, Mount St. Joseph.

*Mom was a strong woman filled with energy, love of family, and a readiness to help those who needed her talents. Over a four-month span in 1982, she kept a simple diary that indicated her feelings, which in turn allowed us to step inside her personality.*

*As I look back, I now see why her daughters and son turned out to be so strong. Because she never learned to drive, she had to depend on others for transportation. At age 73, she loved to walk and was not afraid to take a bus.*

*The family always picked her up to take her to her*
*destination. —S.M.B.*

It was difficult to visit my father in the nursing
home, not only because of the long distance that
separated me, but his mental and physical decline
was so significant. Seeing my Dad like a child in a
grown man's body was devastating.

Memories of him as a strong, loving, fatherly
figure were ripped away whenever I saw him. I
usually cried all the way home, trying to come to
grips with his behavior and physical demeanor. I
knew he was my dad and I loved him. It just seemed
so cruel that this was happening to him.

I kept thinking of all he did for us; the funny
things, the helpful things, and the nice things.
Thanks, Dad.

*Mom's ability to take charge was quite evident each*
*time she visited Dad at the nursing home. If he was not*
*clean, she called the nurse and they cleaned him. If she felt*
*he needed to see Dr. Cummins, she told the nurse to call*
*him. If his clothes were missing, she told the nursing*
*station.*

*She decided to volunteer in their sewing room, as she*
*had worked at St. Vincent Charity Hospital in their*
*sewing room. The nursing home was grateful. This gave*
*Mom the opportunity to be closer to Dad. She came to the*
*home at 8 a.m. to work, ate lunch with Dad, rested in the*
*chair next to him, and then would go back to her sewing*

*until supper, or until one of us would come pick her up in the evening. The family made sure she ate and rested.*

*Mom's boundless energy spilled over to her home. She cleaned walls, closets, the basement, garage, and also went through all of Dad's papers. She sewed and mended clothes for the family, cut the grass, and found time to bowl every week with her sister-in-law Ethel. She often stayed overnight at my sisters' and brother's homes, playing cards and games with the grandchildren.*

*She read the entire paper, watched TV, and said her prayers, always ending the day with her usual expressions of love to God: Wish Dad was home; I love him; God be with him; hope he has a good night; please God, take care of him.*

*The day before he died, she wrote that when she came into his room, he took both of her hands and pulled her toward him and they kissed. The next day, he died at 5:30 p.m. —S.M.B.*

## 1988

Four months before our mother's death, Tim and I had decided it was time to follow our passion and leave Ohio for Cape Cod. It was hard to tell Mom about our plans. We were the first of her children to move out of state. We all cried. Then we talked of her coming to visit us for perhaps a whole month, a couple of times a year. We would have so much fun.

We made plans to move in June 1988. She began to accept our decision to move. In fact, she was even positive and proud that we were following our dreams. We now had two cars and I was able to visit often and would plan visits around Mom's doctor appointments.

*Mom was all packed to leave for a trip to Las Vegas with a senior citizen group. She had her routine doctor appointment on Friday morning. My sister, Barbara Ann, took her, and when they got home, Mom showed her the clothes and jewelry that she had decided to give away, especially rings and necklaces for certain nieces. The doctor said that she was fine and should go on the trip. That night, she called all of us to say goodbye and to tell us that Dr. Cummins said she was fine and should go to Las Vegas. After she called me, she said she was calling my brother, Michael.*

*The next morning, my brother called me to ask where Mom was, as she did not answer the phone. I said, 'Didn't she call you last night?' He said, 'No.' I immediately drove over to see what was the matter. Sister Eileen Quinn came with me.*

*When we arrived, Mary, the neighbor next door, was waiting for me. She said Michael had called her to see what was the matter. Mary said the lights were all on and she could hear the TV. The screen doors were all locked.*

*I walked over to Stanley Bohinc's home and asked him to come and help us get into the house. He broke the lock on the screen door. I used my key but the dead bolt prevented the door from opening. He broke one of the small windows on the door to reach in and unbolt the lock.*

*Mom's chair was empty but the lights were on and her book and glasses were on the table. The TV was on. I went upstairs – no Mom. I went downstairs to the basement – no Mom. Mary checked the downstairs bathroom and found Mom sitting on the floor. By this time, Michael had arrived and called Mr. Mullally, a friend of the family who was a funeral director. Michael also called Anna Mae, Barbara Ann, and Arnie, my brother-in-law.*

*Dr. Cummins examined her and said she must have fainted and her heart had stopped. She had no pain or suffering. Her medicine was on the table in the living room in front of the TV.*

*After Mom's body was taken to the funeral parlor, we all sat down and planned the funeral. We all knew Mom was at peace. She always prayed to die quickly and peacefully and not be a bother for the family or to be in a nursing home. Her prayers were answered. —S.M.B.*

I remember that day in March when she died. I arrived at the family home to take our mother to her doctor's appointment; we didn't need to grocery shop because of her upcoming trip, and she knew I was in a rush to get home. I hustled through the screened door and into the living room.

She stopped and said, "Honey, I want to show you some things." Up the stairs we went and into her bedroom. She pulled out one of the drawers and began to show me several pieces of jewelry that were wrapped in pretty handkerchiefs.

I stood waiting and recalled how, when I was a pre-teen, I would sneak upstairs and look in these same drawers for anything interesting. I was always curious and I still am. I lowered my eyes and confessed to what I had done as a child.

She looked at me and smiled. "I knew you did it." We laughed a laugh that only a parent and child can experience when sharing a memory.

We talked about her legal will and where it was stored and how she's slowly getting rid of things so it would be easier on the family and me. I listened, even though I didn't want to think of her dying. That night, when she called me, I said I had fun going through the drawers with her. We laughed again and said we loved each other. I often think about that day. My Mother must have had a sense that her time was coming soon.

**1992**

Arnie Ruszkowski was married to our sister, Patricia. After her unexpected death in 1976, he began raising their three children by himself. Oftentimes, Sister Barbara and I spoke of how lucky Arnie was when he met his second wife, Felicia Vichill.

We both thought that Patricia was looking down on all of them and somehow directed Arnie on a path where he would meet Felicia. She was a widow with four young teenage sons. Together they joined families into one home filled with laughter, tears, frustration, growing pains, and tons of love.

Arnie suffered from heart disease and passed away in 1992 at 53 years of age. He was active in Boy Scouts and had earned the Silver Beaver Award, the highest honor an adult can receive in Scouting. He was a good father and friend. His children and many others miss him.

## July - August 2000

Our brother's wife was ill with cancer. Nancy was only fifty-four years of age.

Letter from our brother Michael to Sister Barbara and me, July 2000:

> *Sitting in an almost dark room trying to type by touch. Nancy sleeping. 8:20 p.m.*
>
> *Happy 4th to all of you… hope sales are good. I suppose Sr. Barbara told you what's going on here. Briefly…Week ago this past Thursday, Nan woke up and could not see out of her right eye. We spent the day calling to make appointments with docs and then went to see an ophthalmologist in Parma, who sent us to see a surgeon in Cleveland Hts. He kept us there till late eve and ended up sticking needles in Nan's eyes to remove samples and to inject antibiotics into eye.*

*From there, on Friday, we went to Akron for an already scheduled cat scan in AM. A new series of chemo in the afternoon and another round with the surgeon. Saturday — more bad stuff in eye, stayed at the hospital in Cleveland overnight. Took ambulance to Cleveland Clinic for a 3½-hour surgery thru the back of the eye. Then to recovery via ambulance to Akron city Hospital where we still reside.*

*What's happened since? Nancy has been on a constant barrage of antibiotics that changes often for the first week while they determine what bug is causing all the problems. Turned out to be Lysteria. Only about 15 recorded cases of this ever happens anywhere in the eye.*

*Status as of today. No vision in eye expected. Needs a three-hour surgery which she can't have because of immune system not working up to par. Liver not working for last two to three weeks has caused Nan to go from 118 pounds on Thursday when she woke up with no vision to 158 pounds as of yesterday. All in the stomach and legs. We will be here into the weekend, we think. Chemo starting to bring liver back slowly.*

*Nan not feeling right about putting herself through all of this.*

*MICHAEL E.*

Their daughter, Kristen, was going to be married on Cape Cod the following month in August of 2000.

Letter from Michael to Sister Barbara July 8, 2000:

*Kristy came down a couple of hours ago. Visited about 40 minutes. Nancy very happy to hear about the goings on with Kristy's wedding and other stuff.*

*When I came back from walking Kristy to the elevator, Nan was crying… lots…visits tire her out (talking) and thinking and seeing Kristy makes her sad. She will not be going to the wedding. Best not to visit. She says visits are good for the visitor but bad for her, and right now we have to think of her first.*

*Michael. E.*

Our sister-in-law, Nancy, and my brother listened to the wedding ceremony via a cell phone on August 3, 2000, when her daughter Kristen was married.

Nancy died on August 9, 2000. All of her children were beside her, along with Sister Barbara and my brother.

Who was Nancy? As the loving wife of our brother, mother of seven children, and caregiver for many; she was also an outstanding nurse and humanitarian. Initially, she was the Director of

Nursing and, ultimately, the Chief Operating Officer of Grace Hospital. She designed programs that provided vital benefits for thousands of patients and saved many lives. But her family was her greatest joy.

Today, our brother has no interest in finding anyone to share his life with, only his children and grandchildren. He's told me that there will never be another Nancy for him. To this day, Michael tends to chronicle any event or major occurrence around the year that his beloved Nancy died. I always look forward to when he visits with us on Cape Cod or when I return to Ohio to visit with him.

## 2003

In December, we lost another sister, Anna Mae. I was still living in Massachusetts. Tim and I, along with our two Cape Cod babies, left for Ohio to visit her in early November; it was to be our last goodbye.

She greeted us at her door. She hugged me with her free arm, while holding onto a movable metal pole with the other hand. Long, clear tubes that pumped life-saving liquids into her body were connected to the pole.

I held back my emotions. At first, I didn't want my two newest little ones to see her. Her face was so puffy, with one side of her cheek sunken in a bit. But it was her laughing eyes that changed my mind.

They reflected the real joy of my sister to me and to those around her.

We sat in the living room and began to talk. I did most of the talking; it was difficult for Anna Mae to speak. Cancer and multiple surgeries had caused the removal of part of her tongue, which is still a mystery, because she never smoked or used any kinds of tobacco.

It was so good to see her. We laughed a lot. I still miss her weekly phone calls.

*My sister, Anna Mae, at sixty-four years old, mother of five grown children and fifteen grandchildren, is slowly dying of cancer. She is coming to the end of her very active, creative, loving journey of life. She smiles and greets visitors, she is breathing better with a trach tube and she is gaining weight as the feeding tube is helping by not losing any nutrients.*

*She is finally sleeping for six to seven hours at night, on the couch, with Tony at her side. I asked him where he sleeps and he said, "Wherever Ann does." He is a retired CPA and is now the CEO of the Development Office of the Cleveland Diocese. He has become a great caregiver. A hospice nurse comes five days a week and Tony is there all the other times. I go once or twice a week or when needed. My mom always said that Tony was a great person. She was happy when they found each other and married.*

*On November 9, 2003, my youngest sister, Barbara, came from Cape Cod with her family. We are planning to visit with them from 2-4 p.m. and then return to the convent for supper with other family members. I am grateful for family, friends and my faith. All three have stayed with me on my journey, with support, good advice and much love.* —S.M.B.

On December 8, Father John Murphy, a friend of the family, came to visit the Langs. Tony had called everyone home the day before. Jim and Anne with their family, arrived from Massachusetts at midnight on December 9. Anna Mae was waiting for them.

The family gathered around her bed. They prayed the Our Father and Hail Mary. She then fell asleep. After about 5 minutes, Tony said, "I think your mother wants you to all go to bed."

Anna Mae continued to sleep for the next five days, at peace and with no pain. Her family and friends took turns sitting with her day and night. On Sunday December 14, 2003, at 6 p.m., Tony called everyone into her room. We all made a circle around her bed and as we prayed again, her eyes opened and then she fell asleep for the last time.

Anna Mae often told us over the last three months to live one day at a time, that life is fragile and filled with miracles. Be grateful for each moment and remember we have all made each other what we are today. Love your family and your friends as yourself...and always with a good sense of humor.

*We are the work of God's hands, God's heart. Anna Mae was definitely, "God's Work of Heart." She never gave up, as God never gives up on us.* —S.M.B.

## CHAPTER FOURTEEN

## FRIENDSHIP AND DEVOTIONS

*I try to stay in touch with my best friend, Jesus. He has cared for me along the way…although I often did not pay attention.* —S.M.B.

*A* second cousin once described Sister Barbara. "…a woman who walks by faith determined to spread the Good News by her deeds and kind words."

*Jesus is human. He wanted to be human. He had male and female friends. He wanted us to be simple, to speak the truth, to listen to others, to love one another, to respect one another, to know that all are one but diverse. He had a sense of humor. He wanted us to live for others.*

—S.M.B.

*Love and Life are gifts from God. Be a comfort to those who are hurting. Be a good friend. Be kind.* —S.M.B.

When we started the school year, our mother would say, "Notice the children in the schoolyard who have no one to play with, and go over to him or her and play with them." This sometimes felt like a curse but it taught all of us to be friends with everyone.

*Next to family, we need friends to grow. My mom and dad had many friends. These relationships kept them alive and well throughout trials and tribulations.* —S.M.B.

Sister Barbara has always spoken of her wonderful friendships with the Ursuline sisters. They were always by her side when the journey was difficult or lonely.

*Mother's Day. It was a chilly 45 degrees; most people wore coats in church. Father gave the mothers a blessing and a flower.*

*After church, I drove to Calvary Cemetery with Sister Patricia Kukwa. We have been visiting our mothers' graves for over twenty years on Mother's Day. When we lived together, at Our Lady of Peace, we found out that their graves were across from each other. Sister Patricia's mom died in 1986 and my mom died in 1988.*

*On this Mother's Day, there was plenty of sunshine and a cool breeze. When I arrived home, I called my brother Michael. He was walking his dog Sadie. His son Matthew was picking up his younger brother at the airport and they would all be at their sister's house later in the day.*

*I ate my lunch, wrote some letters and felt quite lonely. I waited until 4 p.m. to call at the house and got to speak with all of them. I was not lonely anymore! I know God told me to wait for the right time to call. — S.M.B.*

## Devotions

Sister Barbara absolutely loves Jesus, especially the Eucharist. She feels it energizes her and brings a quiet serenity to her thoughts and whole body. You can feel this peaceful love as she reaches out to the people around her. She literally glows when she talks about Him.

*When I was in grade school, my father would not let me receive Holy Communion if I had been naughty the day before. He often made me eat breakfast to break my fast from midnight, as required by the Church law, so that I could not receive Holy Communion at the 8 a.m. school Mass. I often cried.*

*Later, as a postulant in the Ursuline Community, daily Mass was early, before breakfast. At Communion time, the oldest sisters went first and the postulants were last.*

*The old chapel at Villa Angela Motherhouse had a long white railing, separating the sanctuary from the* people. The railing was divided into two sections with an opening in the middle to walk up to the altar. Coming up the middle aisle to receive Communion, you always walked to the right, all the way to the end, and filled up the railing from right to left. After you received Communion, you would walk back to your place in the benches. There were 16 postulants, eight knelt first while the others stood and waited.

On this particular morning, I landed directly in the open space of the railing. The priest gave Communion to the sisters kneeling and thought I was part of their group kneeling. So, he turned back to the altar and did not give me Communion; thinking I was the last one. He did not realize that I had not received Communion.

I returned to my bench not knowing what to do. On the way to breakfast, I began to cry. Breakfast was in silence, so I could not tell anyone. After breakfast, we had free time until our first meeting of the day. I went to the bathroom to cry. Some of the postulants met me and asked what was wrong. I could not speak.

They called Mother Cecelia, our novice mistress, and told her I was crying. She thought my Grandmother Rose was dying, as she was very ill at the time. Mother Cecelia took me to wash my face. I tried to explain why I cried. I felt so foolish. She apologized and said she was sorry it happened, but Father had already left. —S.M.B.

Growing up as Catholics, we had several other traditional devotions. There would always be a cross of blessed palms tucked behind a framed picture. At the next Easter, there would be new blessed palms, and the old ones would be given back to the church or burned; never thrown away in the garbage.

During Lent, a fasting of forty days before Easter, we, as a family, would kneel in the living room at 8:00 p.m., once a week, and say the rosary out loud, accompanied and led in our prayers via a radio broadcast. At this time, there would also be no meat eaten on Fridays.

A favorite phrase of our mother's when she was surprised was, "Jesus, Mary, and Joseph!"

Whenever we left the house, our mother would always say to us, "God go with you." If we were driving in a car she would add, "St. Christopher protect us." St. Christopher is the protector of travelers.

Today, I find myself saying aloud the same phrase to whoever is in the car with me as we venture off on a car ride. Recently, when I joined my youngest daughter, Annie, along with her husband, Eric, and their foster son, James, on a road trip from Massachusetts to Ohio to visit Sister Barbara, my daughter said the travelers blessing before I had a chance to say it.

# Chapter Fifteen

# Retirement

*As an Ursuline educator of over 50 years, I have been able to view the world with a sense of childlike wonder and the wisdom of a sage. With God's grace and the good health He has blessed me with, I am grateful. I know there is a place for my ministry and gifts, no matter what my age. Who knows what God has in store for me?*

*Many of our Ursuline sisters have passed away or retired. Soon and very soon, I, too, will join their company. Retired religious are just like all elderly in our society. They continue to be vital members and valued contributors to our world.*

*Aging is clothed in mystery. It can confuse us, and it can surprise and astonish us. For some, growing old is a wonderful thing, but for many more it is a great concern. St. Angela Merici told us to get ready for surprises…it is a way to hope. —S.M.B.*

I recall the day she told me about her meeting with the Ursuline Community, in the spring of 2014, about the fate of her ministry. I heard an angry, irritable voice over the phone. I wasn't sure if she was aware that her retirement was going to be the topic of discussion during the meeting with her superiors. My guess is that she defended herself and asked that her ministry continue, but to no avail.

*April 2014 Palm Sunday*
*The hardest aspect of my Lenten time is my retirement. I have to let go of my current ministry. I have felt abandoned and alone. I hope to have the time and the wisdom to use the time and say Thank You to my God. Forgive them for they know not what they do.*

*Monday of Holy Week*
*I hope God will lead me to a peaceful transition within my ministry. I will be quiet and listen with my heart. I can be more attentive to Jesus' presence by smiling at one another, going slow, and taking time. I need to turn over my anger to Jesus.*

*Tuesday of Holy Week*
*God's glory shines through me with my smile as I walk slowly and practice loving Jesus in others. I pray: cleanse me of my anger.*

*Wednesday of Holy Week*

*I still need to overcome my anger. I need to give away my ministry completely. In the next three days, I hope to use God's time, his wisdom, and my gratitude. When I make a mistake, I must go on and be more careful and gentle.*

## Thursday of Holy Week

*O Lord, grant me a peaceful transition by using your time with your wisdom. I show my thanks to Jesus for this gift of life to me by smiling.*

## Good Friday of Holy Week

*Help me to learn from suffering and to deal with the pain in my feet and early retirement. I feel like the crowds watching Jesus on his way to the cross. I must be a light for others and not darkness.*

## Saturday of Holy Week

*May I be a light in darkness and notice the blessings of retirement this Eastertime is bringing me. Also in the friends you have sent me and are sending me right now.*

## Easter Sunday

*Smile at one another. Don't worry. God will roll away the stone and change my mind. —S.M.B.*

I knew it was difficult for her to accept this request of retirement from the Ursuline hierarchy. She assumed she would teach and go on forever, like we all do as we face aging. It took a while for Sister

Barbara to accept the fact that after fifty plus years of teaching little children and working so hard to establish the Ursuline Family Care Program, now in its 20th year, she would have to give it all away.

The good Ursuline Sisters told her the program was so powerful and served such a great need in the community that they wanted it to continue. But her age of 79 was a strong factor. They did not want the program to be lost due to her illness or bad health as she aged.

In her denial and anger, Sister Barbara misinterpreted the Ursulines request of her giving up. It blinded her to what was really happening. It took Sister Barbara three months to understand what they were offering to her.

Eventually a plan was finally decided upon that would include Sister Barbara as part time. During this one year of transition, she would organize all the legal paperwork and files of the Family Care Center, to oversee a smooth changeover. On June 1, 2015, Sister Barbara officially retired from her teaching and ministry. The Ursuline Family Care Program, located at St. Jerome School, was saved. It is currently alive and prospering. As Sister Barbara often says, "God works in strange ways."

*Whatever is in the future for me will happen despite me. But if it is not of God, it will not be. All your carefully laid out agendas and plans must be cast aside. Do not wait until everything is in perfect order. You must be willing to live without certainty!*

*Have FAITH!!*

*God is with us and is working with us. Perhaps instead of complaining, we could try asking a question. 'Here we are Lord. I'm glad you are in charge and not me. What's next?'*

*Lord, help me to accept my situation and let me see your hand in it.* —S.M.B.

# CHAPTER SIXTEEN

# MINISTRY

*S*piritual Ministry is the work or vocation of a minister of religion; the spiritual work or service of any Christian or a group of Christians: the action of ministering to someone.

Sister Barbara has always placed her 'ministry' next to her love for Jesus. This blessed work appears in every chapter of her life and continues to be strong in her daily life, even today.

After moving multiple times over years, from a large motherhouse (the principal residence for a religious community), to convents across Cleveland, to several rented houses, and back to the Ursuline Motherhouse in Pepper Pike, Ohio, Sister Barbara had always looked forward to rekindling friendships formed over her years as an Ursuline sister. Each move was like 'going home' for her.

As of this printing, she is now residing at Light of Hearts Assisted Living in Bedford, Ohio. At 84 years old, she is active and smiles every day.

On my last visit to Ohio, I asked how she felt about moving to an assisted living facility.

She said with a broad smile, "Wonderful! I don't have to take care of a car, worry about buying groceries or picking up my medicine. They even do my laundry and cook all of my meals. I found the puzzle room, Bingo, and am making new friends every day."

I gave her a hug.

"They have Mass and a daily rosary service. In fact, guess what?"

I stood there smiling. "What?"

"I have a new ministry. Every day, I walk the halls on my way to different activities and say hello to everyone. When I meet someone in a wheelchair with their head hanging down, I lift their chin and give them a big smile and say, 'What a beautiful day. God loves you and I'm going to say a prayer for you.' When I pass them again, I see them sitting a little straighter and they're smiling back at me."

*Take my hand and walk with me. Make the most of the time we have and use it to help others that God sends into my life. Oh Lord, let your light reflect in my face to others today.* —S.M.B.

One of the greatest impacts of her ministry was working with children. Listed below are some thoughts from children overheard by Sister Barbara and her teachers.

*...For the little children who are born with enthusiasm, joy, and a sense of the ridiculous, and before we tell them to sit still, fold their hands and keep quiet. Let us pray to the Lord.* —S.M.B.

## St. Joseph Preschool

Thank you for all the time you gave up on us. (Prayer of a child – thanking someone for helping them).

This is my "prettyschool" (meant to say preschool). —Mignon

Katherine is sitting next to Renita (who is bothering her). Katherine tries to straighten a piece of rope. Renita keeps pulling at it. Katherine keeps trying to straighten it and says, "I give up!"

"I'm going to be five on my birthday like Ms. Hayes. Then we will all be five." —Maximilian

"My blood is hurting inside my body."
                                          —Nadiyah

Third grader, Amear and his sister, first grader, Shaunita, came to pick up their cousin, Pre-K Robert. Shaunita was mad because Mr. Z. would not give her paper back until June and her mother will be mad. Amear said, "My sister is working on my last nerve."

Signs of the Times – Child is pretending to talk on a cell phone (he holds a rectangular block to his ear), while working on a puzzle.

Example of positive language – Shakur walks by a table to put his folder away and looked at his friend's picture. "I like your picture." James walks past a child doing a puzzle, "Love your puzzle. You're doing good work."

Terrance said, "My grandmother died. But she won't be dead (buried) until tomorrow."

Mykel ended his work and said, "That's all for me." As he tried to tie his shoes, Mykel said, "I don't have time to fool with this now."

Zsabryan commented, "Sister Barbara, you are clear white and so is Sister Mary."

Comments overheard by teachers and Sister Barbara:

It's so quiet it hurts my ears.

I'm just doing my job!

A little girl is talking on a play phone and turns to a friend, "I would like some privacy."

My Mother is seven and my Dad is twenty.

Pre-schooler, Keonna, celebrated her birthday on Tuesday but when asked how old she was, she said, "I won't be five until my party on Saturday."

My gloves are too little big.

My name is pretty long for a little girl.

My Mommy went to the hairdresser when I was new.

I'm not sleepily!

I know how to spell help: SOS.

My mom and dad have an attitude.

Mommy is staying home and being lazy.

When you sleep, you wake up like new.

I had mushrooms in my hot chocolate.

My Grandma lives by a park but my Grandpa doesn't do parks.

"Sister Barbara, how come you are not a black teacher?"

"Your hands are so white."

"What happens to the stars when it rains?"

"Here, Sister Barbara, please fix this pencil, it's losing its battery."

I have the hookups (hiccups).

I can't sleep, my eyes are too hot.

Two days before Sister Barbara's haircut: "Hey, Sister Barbara, where did you get that big white hair?" and "Why is your hair so fat?"

"When I grow up, I want to be a football team."

After Thanksgiving vacation, the children were asked how long it took to cook the turkey.

Davia said, "Five."

Teacher asked, "Five what?"

Davia said, "Five cooks."

A teacher once said, "Ashley, you are yelling."

Ashley returned with, "I'm preaching."

Children are playing at the dollhouse and repeating over and over, "We don't need a daddy."

On St. Patrick's Day, Bryan arrived in the morning and looked around and wanted to know where the "man" (St. Patrick the man) was.

Two children were cleaning the school by mopping and sweeping. They asked, "Sister Barbara, are we your managers?"

Two boys playing at the dollhouse. One boy said, "I'll be the daddy and you be the fat uncle."

Soniqua was not feeling well (she has asthma): "I have wrinkles in my nose."

Talking on a toy phone, a girl said, "Well, I have to go now. I have to get some things done while my children are sleeping."

René is talking on a play phone and holding it on her shoulder, "Well, you could give it your best shot." As René, all bundled up with her bag on her shoulder, left preschool on a very cold and blizzard day in January, she said, "I can't take it anymore."

Dania sat at a long table coloring her paper, she said to Mrs. Golden, "We can't cheat in Sister Barbara's room. But if we go around the corner, we can."

Sister Barbara asked, "Who was Martin Luther King?"
Cameron answered, "The man who discovered black people."

Sister Barbara said, "You look so pretty today. Did your mommy pick out your clothes?"
Travies said, "Yes! And who dressed you up?"

Conversation between two children:
"I don't have any money."
"Just cost (cough) it up."

Sister Barbara called a child's home.

Jarem answered, "It's my preschool barber (Sister Barbara)."

Mykel's father came to pick him up.
Sister Barbara asked, "Who is this person?"
Mykel answered, "Don't you have a brain? That's my father! He's black and I'm black."

Jasmine lay on the couch in the office to rest in the morning; at naptime, she asked to sleep on 'my desk' (office).

While driving with his mother, a boy said, "Hey, Mom, no cutting! Sister Barbara said so." The mother had got out of line to go around a traffic problem.

In the store at checkout, a man walked in front of the family. The boy said, "Hey, he's cutting, and Sister Barbara said, no cutting!" The man excused himself and went behind the family.

While waiting to be picked up on the last day before Christmas vacation, a little girl said, "I'm tired of going back and forth."

A teacher met a child in the mall with her mother and new baby. The four-year-old said, "When I was this little, I was boring, too."

Kayla moved to a new house and said, "It has a big porch and it's outside."

At 2:00 p.m., the children wake and go to the library. As they enter, they are to pick up a card to sew. Lorenzo kept saying, "I can't do this." A teacher began to help him. The doorbell rang and his uncle came to pick him up. Lorenzo looked up and shouted, "Thank God," as he smiled and ran to the door.

Javeonte asked, "Why do I have holes in my cheeks? Everyone is asking me."

"They are dimples," replied his mom.

"Sister Barbara, how old are you?"

"I'm very old."

"But you have a new face."

"Sister Barbara, you are not black or white. I think you are peach."

In the schoolyard, Tyra was waiting for the bell to ring. I greeted her and told her I was glad she had a sweater. She said, "It's cool in the early."

A little girl wrote on the floor. I told her to go to the office. I asked her why she did that? She said, "My brains fell out." The next day she told me, "My mommy washed my hair and put my brains back in. I'm going to be good today."

Diamond came back to school after missing a few weeks. I hugged her and said, "I missed you." She said, "I missed me, too."

After one week, when the children woke from their naps, a teacher was helping put away the sleeping mats. Tyree stood up, stretched, and said, "I think I am going to like this school." He then looked at me. "You're pretty nice, too."

A teacher told a boy that he was very smart. "I know," the boy said. "It's in my pants!" (Genes)

Two boys were playing in the block room. One of the boys kept knocking the other boys' blocks down. I told the boy knocking the blocks over to stop. He said he didn't do it – his friend did it. I looked at the empty space next to him and said to no one, "Young man, go to my office until you can follow the rules."

The real boy who did the knocking just stared at me and stopped knocking the blocks over.

Ebele was playing with Legos in the Jungle/Zoo area. She took the part of the zookeeper and said, "I have to go to the bathroom." Ebele then switched and became the zookeeper and said, "Okay, but don't forget to flush the toilet and wash your hands."

Four-year-old Traylon was playing in the schoolyard when an eighth-grade boy, almost six feet tall, walked past. Traylon asked the teacher, "How did he do that?" (How tall he was.)

Duane was leaving for the day. It is custom to say goodbye to the child who is leaving. So, we all said, "Goodbye, Duane. See you tomorrow." Duane walked to the door and turned around toward us and shouted, "Do that again." And we did.

A lovely grandmother worked at a book wholesale company. When they threw out PreK books, she would bring them to me for the children. She told her boss, "I know a 'Sister in the Hood' that could use them."

A four-year-old boy told his mother that he knew where Jesus lives. His mother asked, "Really! Where?" The little boy said, "In the bathroom." The boy explained further. "Every morning, Daddy stands outside of the bathroom door and yells, 'Jesus Christ, are you still in there'?"

Words from nieces and nephews:

"Jesus died on the cross, but don't worry, He came back quick! He's okay." —Molly, four-year-old great-niece.

My great-nephew, Owen, is trying to write his name. He took a box of thank you notes and made most of his letters on each card then went around delivering them. I helped him take three of them to hide. He hid Grandpa's behind the TV. After supper, I whispered to him, "Tell Grandpa to look for his card."

So, he brought Grandpa into the room and told him to look around.

I said, "Give Grandpa some clues."

Owen said, "Grandpa, don't look behind the TV."

So much for a four-year-old and clues.

My sister's daughter, Anna, likes to play with the kindergarten children because they are so cute. When asked by her mother, "How about your brother Michael? He's in kindergarten."

Anna said, "Oh no. He's all used up."

## CHAPTER SEVENTEEN

*Monday – day of the moon. The full moon occurs every 29 days, 12 hours, and 44 minutes per month. I always check the calendar each month and find out when it's better to stay home, make no big decisions, and stay calm, if possible.*

*On the day after the full moon, I return to my regular schedule. If I take some time to reflect on what occurred the four days prior to the full moon, I may laugh. But, of course, it was not funny at the time. You may think back to a Monday when you tried to start off on a positive note and everything seemed to go wrong. This, in my experience, proved that the monthly full moon does indeed bring strange happenings to our daily lives. —S.M.B.*

I'm not sure if there was a full moon on the day I decided to co-write my sister's memoir, but my decision definitely steered me onto a new track of thinking. I was successful in writing historical fiction, adding suspense to the chapters, but a memoir? I wasn't sure I could do it because I knew I couldn't make things up or add a character to fix a hole in the story.

But I persevered and thoroughly enjoyed crafting her life together.

Whenever I call or visit Sister Barbara, she usually asks me, "How are you and are the kids okay?" I know she's curious about the progress of the book but, in her wise years, she holds back her questions. She has lived her life with, 'All in God's time.' So, instead of mentioning the book during our conversation, she will subtly say, "Everyone is so excited about my book." Leaving it open for me to discuss if I so choose.

Lately, I've found myself quoting her or using her positive actions as an example when dealing with difficult situations. I never did that before.

Here is one more update on Sister Barbara. She recently moved into the memory center at Light of Hearts Villa where the doors are locked for her own safety.

At first, my brother and I were sad about her confinement, until we discovered that she is still very happy. She continues to greet everyone around her with a beautiful smile. Her face and eyes light up any room she enters. Recently a piano was brought to her floor so she could renew her gift of music and share it with her new floor mates.

The best news is that she reminds us how fortunate she is to be taken care of by her friends, the Ursuline Sisters, and that she always feels safe, warm, cozy, and needed. I know in my heart that her ministry of spreading God's love continues and remains strong.

I'm not sure I've uncovered the reasons behind her decisions to become a religious sister but I have realized that she inspires me every day. I sincerely hope and pray that those of you who read Sister Barbara's memoir will take away at least one idea or thought, maybe more, that will give you hope and faith that things will work for the best, and that God loves you.

## Acknowledgments

by Barbara Eppich Struna

*I* was six years old when my oldest sister Nancy, age eighteen, joined the Ursuline Sisters of Cleveland. They gave her a new name. Over the years, we became known in the family as the 'two Barbaras.' There was always an element of humor when either one of us would call our siblings on the phone and say, "Hi, this is your sister, Barbara," then we had to follow with an explanation as to who was actually calling.

I thought I knew everything about her until she asked me to help write her story.

As I poured over the multiple boxes of her handwritten journals, articles featuring Sister Barbara, and her school awards, citations, and photographs, I discovered a whole new vision of my sister and her role as a religious.

Along this journey of piecing her life together, I've met many strong Ursuline women. I was always amazed at their dedication in serving the underserved. Some would tell their story to me as we ate our meals together, whenever I would visit the convent. Others were modest, keeping their stories to themselves, not wanting to brag.

I thank my parents in heaven for guidance in writing this labor of love. I felt their presence whenever I was stuck on how to organize Sister Barbara's story, or if I should include certain ideas.

A big thank you to members of our family. My brother, Michael Eppich, who was one of my first readers, caught me on some of the details that I thought had happened but, in the end, he knew better. My daughter, Heather, also read the manuscript before it went to print and was pleased to discover some new facts about her aunt, Sister Barbara.

My sister-in-law, Felicia, gave her stamp of approval for some of the family history.

My Wednesday and Friday writing groups assisted in correcting the cohesiveness of the manuscript and my editor Nicola Burnell.

Lastly, my dear and loving husband, Timothy Jon, who would visit me in my office as I wrote, always encouraging to me to keep going, reminding me not to worry about dinner; he'd make something quick for the two of us. Thank you again, Mom and Dad, for giving us all a wonderful life filled with laughter and faith. It was a pleasure to create this gift for posterity and especially for my sister, our family and so many friends.

# ABOUT THE AUTHORS

**Sister Barbara Eppich O.S.U**. is an Ursuline sister and educator, teaching Pre-K and elementary children within the Cleveland Catholic diocese for over 60 years. Sister Barbara holds a B.S. and Master's Degree in Education along with certification as a Montessori teacher.

She has been the recipient of over a dozen grants and numerous civic awards in her community. She was the founder and director of the St. Joseph Family Care Program in Collinwood, Cleveland, Ohio, a Pre-k for four-year-olds. The school relocated in 2010 to St. Jerome School and became The Ursuline Family Care Program.

Her added interest and training in music and liturgy led Sister Barbara to become actively involved in the music ministry of the many parishes she served over her lifetime as an educator, administrator, musician, liturgist, song leader, choir member, and sacred dancer.

**Barbara Eppich Struna,** international best-selling author and storyteller at heart, crafts her tales based on her own personal experiences. She has three suspenseful, historical novels in her Old Cape Series. She is a member of International Thriller Writers, Panelist Thrillerfest 2016; Member in Letters, National League of American Pen Women; President of Cape Cod Writers Center; Sisters In Crime, National, New England, LA. and writes a blog about the unique facts and myths of Cape Cod.

She has written several suspenseful historical novels available as Paperback and ebook through Amazon, B&N, iBook, and independent booksellers.

# ALSO BY BARBARA EPPICH STRUNA

*The Old Cape House*

*The Old Cape Teapot*

*The Old Cape Hollywood Secret*

40406976R00104

Made in the USA
Middletown, DE
28 March 2019